THE
EARLY CHILDHOOD
TEACHER'S
Almanack

activities for every month of the year

Hundreds of UNIQUE IDEAS and Suggestions of a Most Practical Nature for the Teacher

Field Trips, Recipes, Classroom Environments, Arts/Crafts, Games

by
Dana Newmann

illustrated by
Sarah Laughlin

The Center for Applied Research in Education

© 1984 by

The Center for Applied
Research in Education, Inc.
West Nyack, New York 10995

Eighth Printing . . . . . February 1988

Library of Congress Cataloging in Publication Data

Newmann, Dana.
    The early childhood teacher's almanack.

    Includes index.
    1. Creative activities and seat work—Handbooks,
manuals, etc. 2. Activity programs in education—
Handbooks, manuals, etc. I. Title.
LB1537.N48 1984   372.5   84-12726

ISBN 0-87628-287-7

Printed in the United States of America

To
Ethel Maxine Baughman-Arter
who gifted her children
with the idea that:
You can do anything you set
your mind to.

With much love.

ABOUT THE AUTHOR

A graduate of Mills College in Oakland, California, Dana Newmann has been an elementary teacher and reading specialist for more than 10 years. Her experience includes teaching in the public schools of Monterey and Carmel, California, with the U.S. Army Dependents Group in Hanau, West Germany, and at Albert Schweitzer College in Switzerland. In addition, Dana has served as the Reading Specialist for the New Mexico State Department of Education.

Mrs. Newmann has written several books for elementary teachers, including *Individual Discovery Activity Cards* (The Center, 1974-75), *The Teacher's Desk Companion* (Macmillan, 1979), and *The NEW Teacher's Almanack* (The Center, 1980).

The author presently lives in Santa Fe, New Mexico, with her husband and daughter, and teaches at Little Earth School, a private preK and elementary school.

ABOUT THE ILLUSTRATOR

Sarah Laughlin is a cartoonist who lives in Portland, Oregon. She draws and works at the Bread and Ink Cafe, which she built with friends and family.

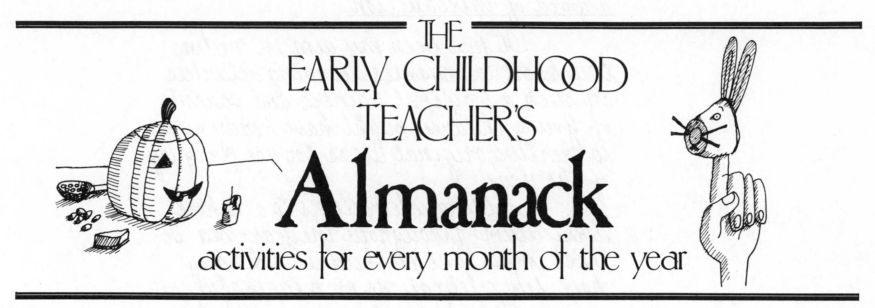

THE
EARLY CHILDHOOD
TEACHER'S
Almanack
activities for every month of the year

a word of introduction

It has been my aim in writing this book to organize learning activities in such a way that teachers and parents of young children might have ready access to creative, original ideas for use everyday of the year.

Adding celebrations to a school curriculum - throughout the year - can be most important to children who may have few celebrations or meaningful rituals in their lives. It is, of course, not practical to attempt to note each year every special day I've included; it will be fun to try some of the activities you didn't use this year when next year rolls around...

The seasons are emphasized in The Early Childhood Teacher's Almanack, with particular attention to the world of nature. Each month includes information and ideas related to common birds, animals, insects, plants and trees.

Other activities deal with the elements: water, snow, sun and wind, and with our five senses.

Every month features recipes that young children can prepare, field trip ideas and easy to make environments including a castle, a rocket ship, private spaces, a diving bell, a teepee and "another planet." Directions for creating holiday keepsakes is a unique feature of this Almanack.

The arts and crafts projects make use of common easy-to-obtain materials including spools, paper bags, milk cartons, string and buttons. There are lists of enrichment objects and addresses from which the more unusual (skulls, ethnic cooking utensils) may be obtained. Such enrichment materials are especially beneficial for young children to investigate or use.

Special days are introduced in story form and all background information is worded in simple terms that preschoolers will easily understand.

Yolanda Carbajal, a co-worker at Little Earth School, and an outstanding preschool teacher, has kindly reviewed this book and she noted that:

"My experience has been that young children understand history only as much as they can touch it, taste it, smell it, hear it, see it; focusing on the self validates their world view and may help them grow _beyond_ their self centered ness." The celebrations in this book are offered as cultural, rather than religious expressions. Cultural celebrations give us opportunities to share special customs, and ethnic foods. As a teacher, try to involve the children's parents and grandparents in school celebrations, whenever possible. Help your children to recognize the ties between generations, the ways in which we may serve, help, and share our affection with others.

And that is the aim of this book: to help you involve your youngsters with other playmates, with fresh ideas, and with the world around them too.

Dana Newmann

TABLE OF CONTENTS

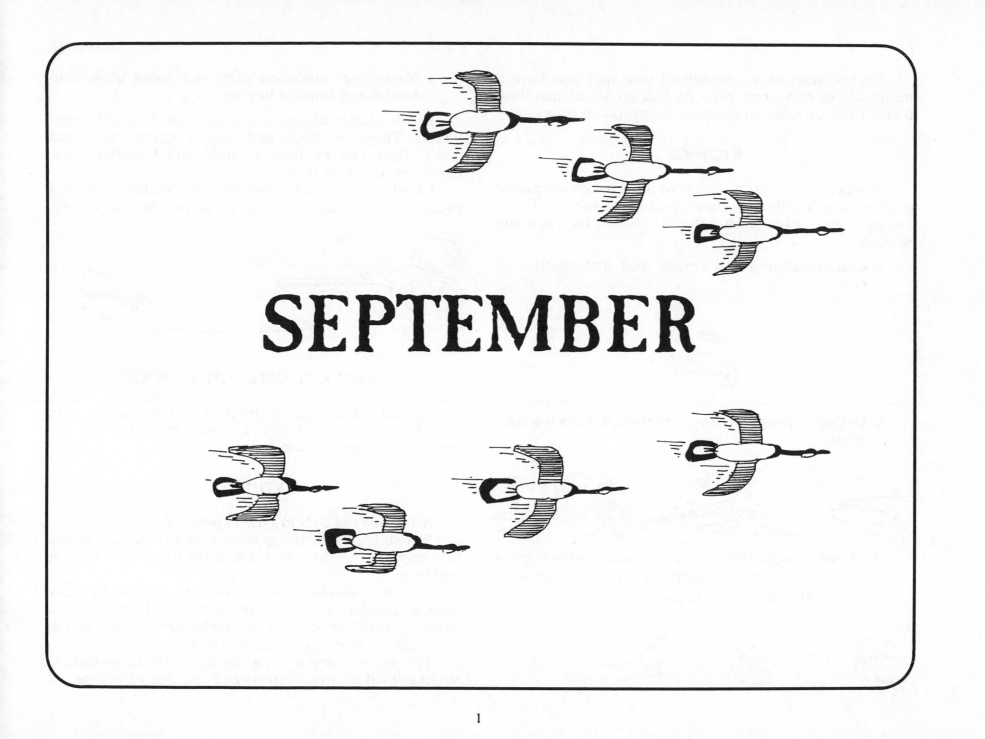

SEPTEMBER

It's the start of a new school year and you have a multitude of concerns. How do you go about handling them? Here are a few suggestions to get you on your way …

STORAGE

Storage is a concern. Ask your local ice cream parlor to save some 5-gallon ice cream containers for you. These can each be used to store materials needed for a specific project.

1. Construction: wood scraps and little bottles of glue

2. Collage: paper scraps, cardboard backing and paste

3. Stamp-design: ink pads, paper, and rubber stamps
4. Sewing: burlap squares, thick yarn, #4 blunt plastic needles, and large embroidery hoops

5. Modelling: plasticine clay and some objects to model and imprint in clay

Large plastic dishpans are also good storage containers. They are strong and easy to stack, carry, and clean. They can be used to hold small stuffed toys, blocks, or building toys.

Label your storage shelves with pictures so that young children may put away scissors, glue, paper, etc.

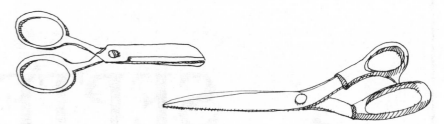

BLOCK-CONSTRUCTION PLAY

Spread a throw rug on the floor when children build with blocks. This will deaden the noise and serve to localize the construction area.

BIRTHDAYS

A birthday is a child's own special day.

Marking each birthday with a small celebration is a fine way to show love and recognition for each of your children.

It's fun to develop a few birthday traditions. You may have a wonderful rhinestone tiara (purchased from a costume, thrift or window display supply house) which may only be worn by a birthday child.

Perhaps you will serve a special Applesauce Cake—alight with the correct number of candles, of course.

Applesauce Cake

Beat together until smooth 1 cup honey and ½ cup butter. Beat in 1 egg. Sift together ½ teaspoon salt, 1½ teaspoon soda, 1 teaspoon cinnamon, ½ teaspoon cloves, and 1¾ cup cake flour. Stir these into butter mixture until smooth. Heat ¾ cup applesauce. Beat into the batter. Bake in oiled 9-inch tube pan in 350° oven for 40 minutes. (To vary cake you may add 1 cup raisins or 1 cup chopped walnuts or 2 tablespoons carob or cocoa.)

Often a funny little Play-Doh cake (with holes on top into which the child inserts his or her own candles) is all that is required to please a very young child.

A special paper hat (see the May section) for the celebrant may also add to the festivities.

You may ask the other children to each draw a special picture for the birthday child or you may give her or him a traditional gift, e.g., a very special pencil sharpener or helium-filled balloon or a surprise ball. You can make up 5-6 of these at a time and so be prepared for upcoming celebrations.

Birthday Surprise Balls

You will need yarn of various colors, crepe paper of various colors, tiny trinkets, toys, and prizes purchased from craft, dime, toy, party or display stores. These may include tiny figures, cars, rings, pins, balloons, rubber spider or worm, little airplanes, pencil, tiny finger puppet, whistle, watch, or metal ring puzzles. Brand new pennies are also popular.

Tie "the best" prize to one end of a piece of crepe paper or yarn. Wind the yarn around the prize, forming a ball. Every few feet tie another toy or prize and continue winding. When the yarn length runs out, tie a new color to it and continue making the ball, incorporating 5-7 surprises in the finished crepe paper or yarn ball. Every child will love unraveling such a special birthday treat!

POSTER PAINTS

Mix tempera paints ahead of painting time. Use a small funnel to help you transfer each color into a clear plastic detergent bottle. Now you can quickly find the colors you need (you can mix by simply shaking bottles) and they are easy to control and are non-breakable!

Young children can learn to mix their own paints by following a recipe (that is "written" in pictures):

3 T. powdered paint
3 T. liquid starch
1 T. water

SOME PLAYING DRESS-UP IDEAS

A large old trunk can be outfitted for hours of "let's pretend" fun. Here are some things to include in the trunk.

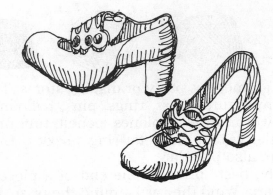

Quick-to-make shirts of colorful remnants afford hours of quick-change fun. Simply fold over the top two inches of 1-yard length of fabric. Then stitch the two short sides of fabric together. Run a piece of flat elastic through the top overlap, stitch the ends of elastic together, and voilà! You have a dress-up shirt!

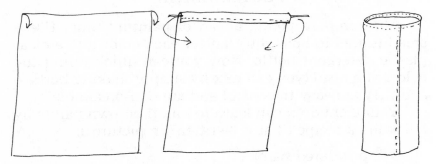

Vests can be made quickly, also. Cut fabric with pinking shears. Seam the two shoulders and add big buttons down the front.

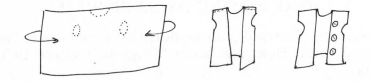

The trunk can include unexpected accessories such as flowery hats, false beards, mustaches, hip boots, a small umbrella, and clear plastic high heels.

Contact the supply room of your local hospital. Ask if you might obtain a used surgeon's shirt/jacket, a nurse's cap, and rubber gloves. Consider outfitting a doctor's old bag with used safe instruments, bandages (made from an old sheet), face mask, paper hats/slippers, tongue depressors, a penlight, and so on.

COOKING AT SCHOOL

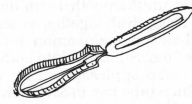

Check with the parents to learn of any allergies your students may have. You will have to keep these in mind, of course, when planning cooking projects.

"Julia Child is a very important and famous cook. Maybe you have seen her on television. Another word for 'cook' is 'chef,' a French word. Julia Child is probably the most famous chef in the world today.

"It takes a lot of patience and care—and a lot of practice—to be a good cook. You're going to get some practice with cooking this year. Maybe *you'll* grow up to be a good chef, too!"

Nutrition should be a foremost objective of cooking projects. By preparing nutritious snacks, children may be exposed to healthy foods and good eating habits. Use whole grains, honey, wheat germ, carob, molasses, and (unsulphured dried) fruits and nuts in all your recipes.

During school hours, adults in the kitchen area should not be involved with boiling oil, water, or syrups. Pans being used on the stove during school time should have their handles pushed to the back.

Before involving the children in a cooking project, read the entire recipe. Assemble all utensils and ingredients. Use long-handled wooden spoons and a BIG stainless steel bowl.

Each child can wear a large T-shirt to protect his or her clothing. Help the children wash their hands first (so that they may handle the dough or any other such foodstuff). Push up long sleeves and tie back long hair using covered rubber bands or narrow strips of cloth.

Go over the recipe with the children so that they understand the steps that are needed to complete it.

(Don't have the ingredients or the utensils on the table during this short discussion as these would be distracting to the children.) Allow plenty of time to complete each step of the recipe, so that no one will feel rushed. Cooking experiences should be pure fun!

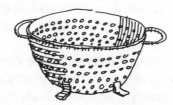

Here it is—*September!* Time to plant bulbs to come up in May ... Time to gather fruits for drying. Summer comes to a close as we begin this new school year!

BETTER BREAKFAST MONTH

Which is the better breakfast?

a. crust of bread and water

b. cake, salt water taffy and orange juice

c. Greek salad and retsina

d. bagel, cheese fruit and yogurt

Of course, you cannot assure each of your children a proper breakfast every morning. (You *can* keep a few oranges and some yogurt and graham crackers on hand for a youngster who arrives without having had breakfast ...) You can also help them become aware of what constitutes a good breakfast (milk, juice or fruit, toast or cereal, egg or peanut butter or cheese) and why a good breakfast is very important. (Your body runs on food, just the way the car runs on gas. Without food, your body acts tired and you feel weak or grumpy. When you get up in the morning, it's been 8 or 9 hours since your body has had anything to run on. It needs to have food to build up your muscles, your bones, and your eyes, and to give you energy for this new day!)

Also let them know why a sugar donut is not a good breakfast. (Sugar gives us quick energy which is good, but this kind of energy doesn't last, so very soon your body feels run-down again. Sugar doesn't help build up your body. You need to drink milk and eat some fruit and eggs to help keep your body strong, and to help keep it going *all* morning long!)

LABOR DAY

Labor Day is the first Monday in September. Explain to the kids that "labor" means work.

Ask your children to name some people whose work helps us everyday. Count how many workers change our lives by their labor or work, such as the traffic patrol people; milk or mail or newspaper deliverers; grocers; teachers; TV, radio, and telephone workers; bakers; garbage collectors; dentists; and nurses—it's a LONG list.

Explain how Labor Day is the one day a year on which we say "thank you" to all these workers for helping us in so many ways.

Mention how some people have jobs that must be done at night. These people sleep in the daytime and work all night. Can your students name some night workers?

Let the children act out a community helper at work. (This may be done during Circle Time.) Try and guess the identity. Always make certain to emphasize that men can be nurses and telephone operators and secretaries, and women can deliver mail and paint houses and repair telephone lines!

CITIZENSHIP DAY

September 17 is Citizenship Day. Five- and six-year olds can understand that a citizen is a person who belongs to a country. Our country is called the United States. Sometimes we call it America.

Today we think about how our country helps us. How do *you* think America helps us? (It keeps us safe and keeps our town and schools running smoothly. The students' answers should be enlightening and, perhaps, humorous.) How can people be good citizens? (By paying their taxes so America can keep going. By obeying laws so we all can be safe.) How can you—and I—be a good citizen? … Let students come up with their own ideas and answers.

One concrete way that they can celebrate today is by doing something about litter. (Look around the room. Do you see any litter right here in our room? Let's be good citizens and pick up this litter. Now let's take a big plastic bag and go on a short walk around the block to see how much litter we can find to pick up. This is one way we can help America stay beautiful and we can practice being good citizens, too.)

THE AUTUMN EQUINOX

Autumn Equinox falls on (or about) September 23. Today is the day we say "hello" to fall. What a perfect day to take a nature walk! Before setting out, get a copy of a field guide to the common trees, flowers, and birds of your area. Familiarize yourself with the names of three or four of the most common plants, trees, and birds so that you can help the children learn to identify (and feel at home with) a few of the forms of nature that they are living near. (Plan each season to take this kind of walk, perhaps over the same route.) Bring along a shopping bag for treasures they find and several hand lenses or magnifying glasses so the kids can study acorns, pine cones, leaves, seeds, and insects up close!

Help the children look for signs of autumn: people raking, leaves blowing, low-hanging clouds, flocks of migrating birds. Encourage them to feel different textures as they walk along. Bring some Play-Doh and press objects into it to make a variety of textural impressions.

Help the kids find special objects and places of beauty. Help them to see the variety in nature—in the textures, colors, patterns, shapes of wood, bone, rusted metal (the "rust" is the natural part)*, bark, plants, feathers, shells. If you find a cocoon or some rose hips, bring them back to class, to observe the former and brew tea from the latter!

Look at the clouds and find animals and objects in their patterns. Do the same with the patterns formed by fallen leaves on the ground, tree bark, dried grasses, stones or sandy areas.

Ask the children to look for specific leaf shapes: a leaf that has saw-toothed edges or rounded edges, or a leaf that looks like a dog, or a ship or a person. Have them collect a variety of autumn leaves. When you get back to school, you can have fun with them. You can:

1. See how many ways (by size, color, shape) the kids can group the leaves.

2. Use map tacks to pin a leaf to a piece of colored paper. Cut a sponge into little squares. Let each child dip a sponge in poster paint and gently dab up and down on the paper all around and overlapping the edge of the leaf. Repeat this process with a variety of leaves. Then talk about the different shapes. Group like shapes together.

---

*The children may collect objects from outdoors and then sort them into 2 groups: organic and non-organic, once they return to school again.

3. Place a leaf, vein-side up, on the table. Cover the leaf with a piece of typing paper. Rub a crayon back and forth across the leaf to make a quick picture of it. Add a light wash of watercolor for a lovely autumn momento.

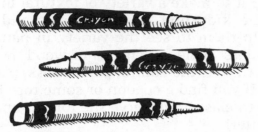

Look for details on your walk: colors (what is the brightest?), sizes (what is getting smaller now that it's autumn? bigger?), shapes (what things change their shapes in fall?). Point out trees that lose their leaves in fall. Look at the ground. What's happening to the leaves on the ground? Now look at the earth! Why does it have bits and pieces of leaves and twigs mixed in it?

Point out a tree that does not lose its leaves in fall. How are the needles changing? Look at the ground. Why do some needles fall off the tree? Notice the pine cones and how and where they grow on the tree.

Another way to enjoy your fall walk is by having fun with numbers and the concept of size. "Here is a stone; it is bigger than this twig and it is smaller than _____." (Let students fill in this blank.) "Take three little steps, turn to your left and take two BIG steps. Stoop down and pick up one twig and four leaves. Put all the leaves in a pile here and all the twigs in a pile to the *right* of the leaves. Let's arrange the leaves in sets (families). Now let's arrange the twigs from smallest to biggest. Finally, let's put all of the leaves and twigs back where we found them. Do you know why?" (so they may return to the earth and feed the soil)

PRESERVING NATURAL ITEMS

If you live in an area that has an abundance of colorful autumn leaves, flowers, and grasses, help the children collect a wide variety of these and bring them back to school. Once there you can try preserving these natural materials!

Dipping in Wax. Although the flowers don't last long, five-year-olds love the magic of this process. You'll need lots of newspapers, flowers with one row of petals, such as daisies (not multiple petals, such as chrysanthemums), a soda bottle for each flower, a 16-oz. coffee can with plastic cover, a big pot of water, and one pound of paraffin wax.

Before the children arrive at school, carefully melt the paraffin in the coffee can which is standing in pot of boiling water. Melt the wax slowly and, once it is clear, turn off the heat. Spread newspaper over every surface on which the children will be working.

Each child dips a flower stem in wax and waits for it to dry. Next, she or he holds the stem and twirls the petals in wax. Then the child gently shakes the petals on a newspaper and places the flower in a soda bottle to cool.

NOTE: If wax should spatter clothing, place an ice cube on the wax. The wax should harden so that you can crack and remove it.

If any wax remains in the coffee can, put the plastic lid on it and refrigerate until the wax is hardened. Then you can put it in the garbage.

Burying in Fine Sand. You'll need a shoe box, very fine sand to fill it, and young zinnias, marigolds and chrysanthemums with 1½″ stems. Don't try violets, petunias or bulb flowers as their petals are too thin. Pour a layer of sand in the box. Stick the flower stems into the sand, leaving room around each flower. Gently pour in more sand until the flowers are covered. Don't touch the box for two weeks. Then gently remove the sand and use a fine brush on the petals.

While you're on your walk, look for some mushrooms or toadstools. These simple fungi are like mold and grow from spores, not seeds. Bring the mushrooms or toadstool caps back to school. Gently pull one of the caps apart and examine the spore plates. Place the caps, rounded sides up, on sheets of white paper. Gently tap the top of the caps. Place a small bowl over each cap. Leave them on the paper overnight. In the morning, remove the bowls and lift the caps from the paper. Spores have fallen from the spore plates and formed a print on the paper!

BIRDS IN AUTUMN

"In the fall many birds fly south to warmer places. Then in the spring, they will come back. We call this migration. Do you know why birds migrate (fly south) in the fall? When it gets cold many birds have a hard time finding food. The seeds and little insects are gone so the birds fly away to a warmer place where they will find food again.

Do you know why geese fly in a V shape when they migrate? They do it so that each bird can see the other geese and they all follow the lead goose who knows the way best."

If you decide to have the children begin feeding the birds, you must be consistent and continue putting out food all winter long. Check the feeder daily. Birds form eating patterns and may starve to death if their food is discontinued in midwinter.

Cater to your particular bird population. Sparrows and cardinals eat just seeds, blue jays enjoy suet, and robins appreciate bits of fruit.

How to Make Homemade Birdfeed

Ask your butcher for some pieces of suet. Let the children tie long pieces of cord around each piece of suet which will then be hung from a convenient branch or window overhang.

Collect pine cones and help the children to roll these in a mixture of peanut butter (or lard) and birdseed. Suspend cones by a thin wire or cord from branches, or even a fire escape.

The Audubon Society offers this recipe: Mix equal parts of melted beef suet and sugar syrup (three parts water and one part sugar boiled together). Cool. Form into 3″ balls. Roll in chopped nuts, seeds or bread crumbs. Chill until hard. Tie the balls from a tree, bush, or window.

Birds need water as well as food. Place a clay draining dish (the kind used under flower pots) filled with water on a feeding tray on the windowsill. The children can then watch the birds bathe as well as drink! If you live in an area where the temperatures go below freezing don't use metal containers for bird baths. The birds feet can freeze to a metal bath! Try a plastic lid to a trash can: this makes a safe cold weather bird bath.

INSECTS IN AUTUMN

Where do insects go when it gets cold? Insects cannot make their own body heat so many insects freeze to death once summer is over. They leave behind many, many eggs and cocoons which will hatch in the spring.

Some insects do live through the fall and winter. Honeybees keep moving and buzzing inside their hives. They make a huge ball by staying close together and moving around to keep each other warm. Bald-faced hornets all die in winter except the queen who goes underground and sleeps until spring. The bumblebee queen does the same thing. Then when it's spring, she comes out and lays her eggs.

Some insects migrate in the autumn just as geese do. The monarch butterfly and the green darner dragonfly both fly south at this time of year.

A few insects are awake and busy all year round. Fleas and lice that are living on birds and animals are kept warm by the feathers or fur that covers them. Insects that live in caves are moving around because it is always pretty cold inside a cave. These insects are used to cool fall days.

AN AUTUMN GAME

Hide a large number of a variety of nuts (peanuts in the shell, walnuts, almonds, etc.) in the backyard or play area. Tell the children to pretend they're squirrels and go outside and hunt for some good winter food. (Have a supply of extra nuts handy for that one player who may not find as many nuts as the rest of the "squirrels.")

NATIONAL DOG WEEK

National Dog Week begins with the Sunday of the last full week of September.

Collect colored pictures of a variety of dog breeds. Discuss why some dogs need long fur, legs, or ears, and others need short ones. (Dogs have had to catch their food in different ways and so different parts of their bodies have grown to help them. Hounds have fast legs to run down rabbits, bassets have short legs to get badgers in their holes. Some dogs, such as huskies, have needed to keep warm with thick fur, and others, like

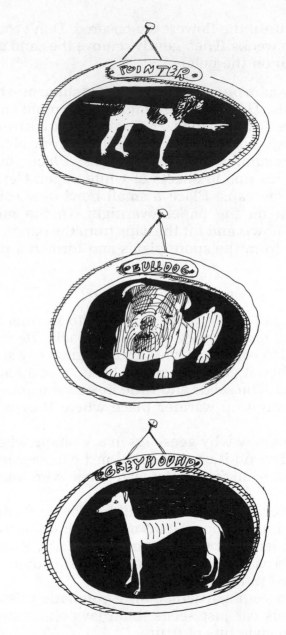

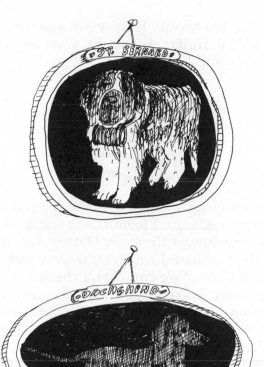

mals. The preschool-kindergarten guide is about $10. Write, requesting current price, to:

> The National Association for
>   the Advancement of Humane Education
> Norma Terris Humane Education Center
> P.O. Box 362
> East Haddam, CT 06423

Chihuahuas, have needed to stay cool by being almost hairless.)

Talk with the children about why a dog is an important animal. (A dog may give you love, keep you company, and help you out of trouble.) Then ask the kids how many of them have a dog at home. Learn the breeds and names of their pets. Ask if they think dogs have feelings. Why or why not?

The National Society for the Prevention of Cruelty to Animals offers a very thorough K-3 curriculum guide for teaching children kindness and empathy toward ani-

Here is a recipe your children should enjoy making by hand:

Biscuits for Dogs (and Cats)*

3½ cups all-purpose flour
2 cups whole wheat flour
1 cup rye flour
1 cup corn meal

---

*This recipe appeared in the very interesting Monterey Church Calendar Cookbook: *The Portly Padre* edited by Dorothy Taugher and available from All Saints' Episcopal Church, P.O. Box 1296, Carmel, CA 93921. This fascinating cookbook is filled with historical anecdotes and recipes alike. Write to request current price.

2 cups bulgur (cracked wheat)
½ cup nonfat dry milk
4 tsp salt
1 pkg. dry yeast
2 cups chicken broth
1 egg plus 1 T milk to brush on top
warm water

Combine all dry ingredients except yeast. In a separate bowl, dissolve yeast in ¼ cup warm water. To this add the broth. Add the liquid to the dry ingredients, mix, and knead 3 minutes. The dough will be stiff. If too stiff, add extra liquid or an egg. Roll out the dough to a ¼″ thickness. Cut into various shapes or let children make little bone shapes. Place on an unoiled cookie sheet. Brush with milk or a beaten egg on the tops. Bake at 300°F. for 45 minutes. Turn off the heat and leave the biscuits overnight in the oven to get bone hard.

AMERICAN INDIAN DAY

There are over 250 different American Indian tribes or groups. Each has its own individual customs, religious ideas, and ways of dealing with the natural surroundings. This is why it is difficult to teach about Native Americans in any generalized terms. Help your kids to see beyond the stereotypical Indian living in a teepee or riding a pinto, and shooting buffalo.

Let the children look at (encyclopedia) pictures of Indians living in Alaska, Florida, Arizona, and Kentucky. Ask them to see how differently Native Americans dress and live in the north and south (and west and east) of the U.S. Then tell them, "We can thank the American Indian for sharing many good things with us. Listen to all the things we have gotten from these people: turkey, corn, squash, chile, beans, and moccasins. You know a lot of American Indian words, too. Can you guess some words we got from the Native Americans? Here are some (more): skunk, teepee, raccoon, squaw, toboggan, tomahawk, moose, hominy, hickory, moccasins, opossum, and chipmunk!"

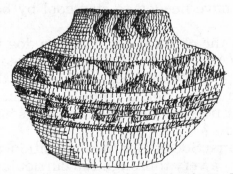

A thousand years ago the American Indians made beads by drilling holes in seashells or stones or pieces of pottery. Then they would string these wampum beads and use them as jewelry AND money. Here is a recipe for sand clay that can be used by your kids to make sand clay beads which, when hardened, resemble prehistoric Indian beads.

Sand Clay Beads

2 cups sifted (tan or rust-colored) sand
1 cup cornstarch
1½ cups cold water

Place in a pot over medium heat. Stir constantly for 5-10 minutes until mixture thickens. Turn out onto a plate, cover with a damp cloth, and cool.

Children can roll out bead shapes, using round toothpicks to make bead holes and to scratch or imprint designs on beads' sides. When made, allow beads to dry for a day, turning them once or twice. String the beads on a cord, interspersing little shells or glass beads between the sand clay beads.

ROSH HASHANA AND YOM KIPPUR

The Babylonians made a calendar thousands of years ago to follow the cycles of the moon. This lunar calendar

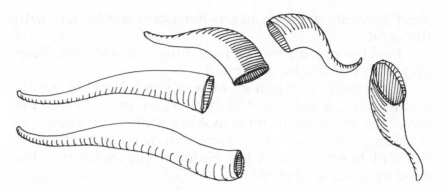

is used by the Jewish people today. That's why the exact dates of Jewish holidays are different each year.

Rosh Hashana, the Jewish New Year, often occurs in September. It is traditional to serve apple slices dipped in honey in anticipation of sweetness for the year ahead!

(Yom Kippur is the Jewish day of atonement and a day of fasting. Although it is unlikely to be noted during your school day, Jewish students may be absent on this day.)

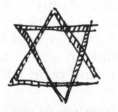

SANDBOX PROJECTS

Provide the children with a large amount of clean dry sand (contained within a hard plastic wading pool or an area deliniated by wooden barriers such as railroad ties). At first just let them dig and use small shovels, spoons, pails, and cups. Watch and see how they relate to the sand and stop any undesired behavior before it gains momentum or attention. Say any rule firmly ("We don't throw sand") and show the child an alternative way to play with the sand.

Provide objects for pouring, filling, and sifting. Keep all toy dump trucks well oiled.

Eventually dampen an area of sand. Provide plastic picnic forks, knives, and large plastic combs so that the kids may experiment with making different textures on the damp surface. A sprinkling can or spray bottle may be kept handy so that the children can redampen the sand as often as they wish.

Indoor Fun-With-Sand Projects

Sand Painting: Sift clean white sand and divide it into several small bowls. Into each bowl mix a different ingredient from the following list: dry mustard, paprika, blue clothes detergent, and instant coffee. (Look around your kitchen for other coloring agents.) Add water and a little white glue to each bowl and then let the children make sand paintings!

Sand-Printmaking: Apply white glue (liberally) to the veined underside of a leaf or fern. Then press the leaf onto a sheet of colored paper, and lift it off again. Sprinkle the glue leaf print on the colored paper with fine white sand and your sand print will appear!

SEPTEMBER FIELD TRIPS

On September 21, 1789, the United States Post Office was established. Contact your local post office to learn if it can offer your children a short tour of the facilities. Request a guide who understands the vocabulary of young children and who may let them touch a few things or give them a just-cancelled envelope bearing today's date!

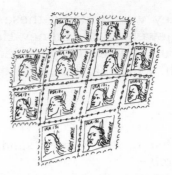

Other appropriate trips to take this month include visiting a bakery in operation (donut shops often offer excellent donut preparation demonstrations), a children's dentist, or a wildlife preserve. Perhaps you might invite a forest ranger to come and talk with your kids.

Look through the Yellow Pages of your phone book to gain ideas for field trips or guest speakers. Simply phone and inquire if it would be possible to bring a small group of children to visit. Ask a parent or two to accompany you on the trips.

ENRICHMENT OBJECTS

Actual American Indian arrowheads are available at minimal prices from:

Southwestern Minerals Inc.
7008 Central Avenue, S.E.
Albuquerque, NM 87108

Write to inquire the current prices or call (505) 268-6778. Each projectile point is authentic and unique.

Consider investing in an actual rattlesnake or beaver skull or the entire backbone of a boa constrictor! While these are not inexpensive, you will use them over and over and children will always be fascinated by them. Snake sheds and small collections of bone samples are also available from:

Herp-Osteo Specimens
3919-A West Magnolia Boulevard
Burbank, CA 91505

Write to request a price list and indicate your special interests.

SEPTEMBER PUPPETS

Children love puppets. They enjoy using them and they never tire of watching them in action. Here are some quickies to make.

Finger Puppet

Use a bit of yarn to tie a 5″ × 5″ piece of cloth around the forefinger. The child may use felt-tip pens to draw the puppet's face. A cotton ball, yarn, or sheep's wool hair can be secured to the puppet's head with white glue.

A Variation on the Paperbag Puppet

Provide children with medium and small brown paper bags. Help them stuff these with newspaper. Insert a short dowel or ruler up into the opening of each sack and tie the bags closed with thick yarn.

Use construction paper and help the kids cut out many different shapes and colors of eyes, noses, ears, mouths, eyebrows, and cheeks. Keep these shapes fairly large. Place each category of shape on a separate cookie sheet or in a shallow box. These containers will help children find what they need once they begin decorating their puppets.

Also provide a shallow box filled with rug yarn, thin strips of cloth, sheep's wool, and raffia.

Now ask the children to select the features and hair for their puppets. Help them glue these to the paper bags.

AN AUTUMN TEA PARTY

If you collected rose hips or fresh mint on your autumn walk, steep these in a pretty teapot and then serve warm tea and slices of fruit or handmade cookies on a chilly autumn afternoon!

Teatime Cookies

    1 cup butter
    3 T honey

2 cups unbleached flour
1 T vanilla
¾ cup finely chopped pecans
grating of fresh nutmeg

Cream butter and honey. Add the remaining ingredients. Shape into ½″ balls and flatten with a spatula. Bake at 350°F. for 10-12 minutes.

A tent (right in the school, if you like) can provide a very private atmosphere for listening to a Navajo coyote story or for sipping your afternoon tea. Here's how to erect your tent.

Fold a blanket in half lengthwise. Run a piece of clothesline or rope beneath this fold. Suspend this rope from either two trees or either side of a room with screw eyes. Tie a length of cord around each of the 4 corners of blanket. Then stretch each cord away from tent (enlarging it), and tie each cord to a brick. Line the tent with soft pillows, rugs, or blankets and let the children enjoy their seclusion.

SEPTEMBER RECIPES

Cooking experiences should be very simple at first. Children can learn to wash fruits and vegetables, shell peas, and spread peanut butter on crackers. The very first recipes they prepare should also be simple, such as adding fruit juice to gelatin, and mixing herbs with sour cream or yogurt as a vegetable dip. Gradually introduce recipes that require more ingredients and/or more steps.

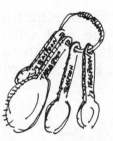

Read over each recipe and adjust the ingredients if necessary. These recipes serve 8-10 children (unless noted) depending on the size of each portion.

Apple Balls

½ cup melted butter   1 tsp cinnamon
1 cup honey   2 cups grated apple
3 cups oatmeal   1 cup finely chopped nuts
1 tsp nutmeg

Boil the honey, butter, and apple for one minute. Make certain the children are at a safe distance. Mix the oatmeal and spices. Add nuts and mix well. Roll the mixture into small balls. Refrigerate for 45 minutes.

Indian Pudding

("This recipe was given to a white woman in 1886 by an Indian squaw," says Mrs. John F. Cooke, 1944.)

3¾ cups milk   4 eggs
1 cup cornmeal   2 T butter
1 cup honey (sugar in   ½ tsp nutmeg
   original recipe)   1 cup raisins
½ tsp salt   ¼ tsp soda

NOTE: Before the children arrive: scald the milk, add cornmeal, and stir constantly for five minutes. Let mixture cool until lukewarm.

Let the children add raisins, honey, beaten eggs, salt, and nutmeg. Bake in a greased pan for 1½ hours at 350° F. If batter stiffens too much during baking, add more milk. Allow pudding to cool a bit and serve it warm (or cold) with a dollop of whipped cream.

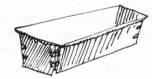

Zucchini Bread

3 cups zucchini (cooked and mashed)
2½ cups honey and 1½ tsp soda
4 eggs
¾ cup oil
3½ cups unbleached flour
½ tsp salt
3 tsp cinnamon
1 tsp each nutmeg and grated fresh ginger
2 tsp each allspice and mace

In one bowl, mix the honey, soda, eggs, and oil until fluffy. In another bowl, add the dry ingredients to the zucchini. Then add this zucchini mixture to the egg batter. (You can also put in raisins or dried apricot pieces or chopped nuts.) Blend 4 minutes, and then pour the batter into 2 loaf pans. Bake at 350° F. for one hour.

You might want to construct a small lean-to in the outdoors and cover the roof with fir boughs if palm branches aren't available. Share a small snack in the sukkah and celebrate Succoth together.

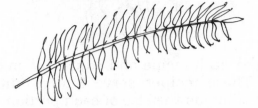

Honey Seed Bars

½ cup honey
1 cup powdered milk
½ cup peanut butter
1 cup sesame seeds
½ cup unsweetened shredded coconut

Heat the honey and peanut butter. Add powdered milk, coconut, and seeds, and mix well. Pat into an 8″ × 8″ pan. Refrigerate until firm (about one hour), then cut into small bars.

SUCCOTH

Succoth (or Sukkos) is a movable feast occurring in either late September or early October. It is a Jewish holiday, The Feast of Tabernacles, and celebrates the fall harvest. Succoth is a reminder to Jewish people of how the Israelites wandered in the desert for 40 years looking for the Promised Land—and how they were forced to live in sukkahs (huts). Jewish people today often build a sukkah in the backyard, making a roof of (palm) branches. For seven nights, they eat the evening meal in the sukkah so that they feel close to those Israelites of long ago.

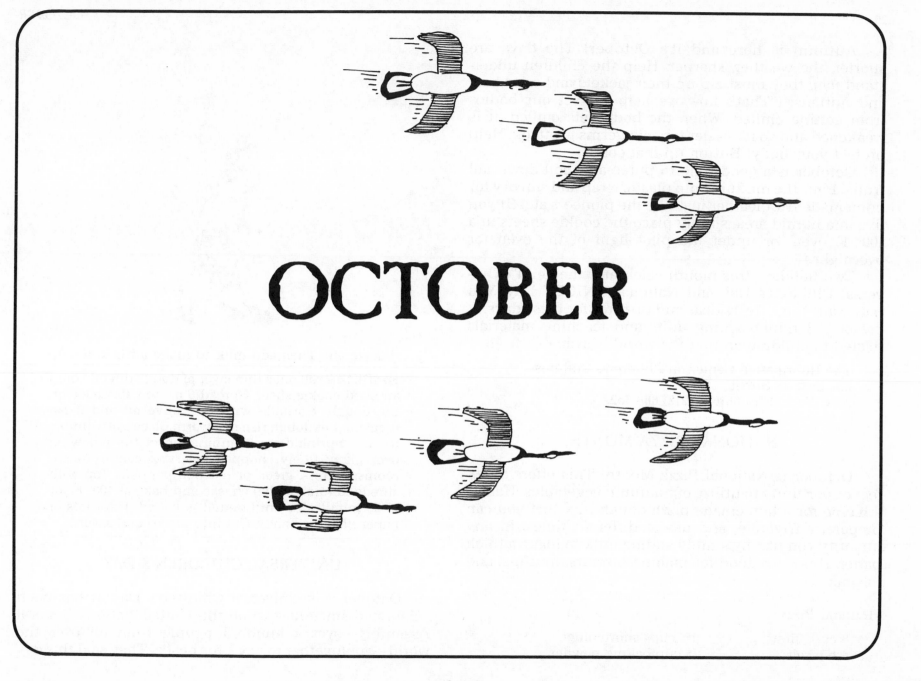

OCTOBER

Autumn is here and it's October! The days are shorter, the weather, sharper. Help the children understand *why* they must zip up their jackets and wear hats and mittens. ("That's how we help protect our bodies from getting chilled. When the body gets chilled, it is weakened and so it's easier for cold germs to attack. Help protect your body! Button up that coat!")

October is a good time to purée and boil down fall fruits. Pour the mixture onto plastic wrap and sun dry for homemade fruit leather just like the pioneers ate! (If you live in a humid area, simply place the cookie sheets in a 100° F. oven, or under the pilot light of the oven for overnight.)

Two holidays this month celebrate "the child": Universal Children's Day and National UNICEF Day. You may want some fresh ideas and pictures for these days. A list of K-3 mini-teaching units and teaching materials related to children around the world is available from:

The Information Center on Children's Cultures
331 East 38 Street
New York, NY 10016   (212) 686-5522

NATIONAL PIZZA MONTH

October is National Pizza Month! This offers a perfect opportunity to utilize our autumn vegetables. Here is a recipe for a homemade pizza dough mix that you can prepare, refrigerate, and use at different times, in any quantity you like by simply adding milk to make a thick batter. It is even good for making biscuits, muffins, and pancakes.

Healthful Pizza

8 cups flour	1½ cups shortening
4 tsp salt	¼ cup baking powder

Refrigerate. Then add milk to make a thick dough.

For PIZZA roll out a thin layer of dough directly onto an oiled cookie sheet. Spread 6 oz. tomato sauce on the dough. Sprinkle with 4 T olive oil and 2 tsp oregano. Let dough rise in a warm place until double in size. Sprinkle any combination of the following over pizza: finely chopped celery, zucchini, mushrooms, carrots, green or red bell peppers. Top with shredded (mozzarella) cheese and bake at 400° F. for 15-20 minutes or until dough is baked. Have lots of paper napkins handy. Cut into pieces and savor!

UNIVERSAL CHILDREN'S DAY

October 3 is Universal Children's Day. It has been celebrated since 1954 when the United Nations General Assembly—over a hundred people from all over the world—got together to work for peace. They said this day should be used every year to help children from all countries get to know and understand each other better.

If you have a UNICEF shop nearby, get a selection of contemporary photographs of children from around the world. The UNICEF calendar has good ones. Kids can learn so much by looking at pictures*; help them identify with the children and activities shown. This is one way to help foster empathy.

FIRE PREVENTION WEEK

This week includes October 8. It's important for children to be aware of both the benefits and dangers of fire.

"A hundred years ago there was a great fire in a city named Chicago. The fire started in a barn and some people said a cow that belonged to Mrs. O'Leary kicked over a lantern in that barn. The lamp fell into the hay and the hay caught fire. Now, there hadn't been any rain in the city of Chicago for a long, long time. Every thing was very, *very* dry. The firefighters tried to stop the flames but they soon spread everywhere. The great fire burned all day and all night and again all day. Houses, stores, churches, bridges—all burned. Many people lost every-

thing they had. That fire happened on October eighth (1871) and so each year we remember it on this day by *thinking* about fires: how to keep them from happening and what to do in case of a fire."

Elicit suggestions from the children for helping to prevent fires. (Don't leave oily dust cloths in a closet. Never play with a lighter, matches, or a gas stove. Make sure a grownup's burning cigarette is not left on the edge of a counter or table.) Talk with the kids about what to do if there's a fire in school. How should we act? (Keep calm. Walk quickly out the nearest door. Why should we all *walk* and not *run*? One of us might fall down and get hurt if we run.) Stress any special safety measures that apply to your school building.

---

*Very young children, who learn about the world best through hands-on activity, may need to be helped to learn "to read" pictures. Start slow: "How do you think the boy in this picture feels? How can you tell? WHY do you think he's feeling so excited? Yes, that's a good guess because there IS a dark cloud up in the sky ... When have *you* ever felt like this: excited and a little scared? ... and so on ... (Thank you, Londi.)

Provide the children with red, yellow and orange paint, large brushes, and big pieces of paper. Let them paint their interpretations of fire burning (the city of Chicago).

Obtain some white moisture-resistant paper from your butcher; it's shiny on one side. Mix liquid laundry starch and red tempera paint and let the kids fingerpaint big fire paintings to decorate the room during Fire Prevention Week.

Fingerpaints

½ cup laundry starch	1 envelope unflavored
1 cup cold water	gelatin softened in
3 cups hot water	¼ cup cold water
(tempera paints)	½ cup Ivory Snow
	Flakes

Combine starch and cold water in a pan. Add hot water. Cook over medium heat until mixture boils and becomes clear. Stir constantly. Remove from heat and stir in gelatin.

Add Ivory Snow Flakes and stir until flakes dissolve. Allow mixture to thicken.

Put 1 T of tempera paint into a jar. (Repeat for each color you may want to use.) Pour thickened starch mixture into a jar. Shake the jar to mix the fingerpaint. Refrigerate when not in use.

CAMILLE SAINT-SAENS

October 9 is the birthday of Camille Saint-Saens (saṅ-sän, as in car). Obtain a record or tape of Saint-Saens' "Carnival of the Animals." Explain to the children how the music is describing each of the animals. Help them to differentiate between the beasts in this piece of music. Then let them have fun interpreting each of the creatures as it appears in Saint-Saens' music.

CHRISTOPHER COLUMBUS

The second Monday of October is Columbus Day.

Have a globe handy so that you can show the children the relative locations of Europe, North America, and India. Read or paraphrase the following story to them. Let them see (encyclopedia) pictures of 15th century sailing ships.

"Over 500 years ago most people didn't know about North America, the place where we live today. There were no cars or airplanes then and not many safe ships. Most people were afraid to travel very far from their homes because they thought dragons or sea monsters would get them!

"Some people in those days thought the world was flat. They thought if you sailed out to sea you would finally just fall off the edge of the world. There was a man, though, who thought he could sail a ship from his home in Europe until he got to India on the other side of the world! His name was Christopher Columbus.

"He tried to get money for a trip to show that you could sail *around* the world to India and come back to Europe bringing wonderful spices and Indian things *with* you. The Queen of Spain believed in him and gave him the money and ships to make the trip.

"Columbus and his men set sail on Friday, August 3, 1492 from Palos, Spain. Columbus had a big ship, the Santa Maria (The St. Mary) and 2 smaller ships, the Pinta, and the Niña. They stopped for fresh water at the Canary Islands. Then they sailed southwest. Twenty-one days later the sailors on Columbus' ships were beginning to feel afraid. They wanted Columbus to turn the ships around and go back home to Spain. Just then they saw a flock of birds! Can you guess what that meant? Well, Columbus sailed in the direction that the birds had come from and at 2 o'clock on the morning of October 12, they saw land! It was the island we now call San Salvador, but Columbus thought it was the Indies, so the new world was called 'the Indies' and the people Columbus found living there he called 'Indians.' (Look on your globe. How much farther off were the real Indies?)

"Columbus stayed and looked around the islands. He got a lot of things together to take as presents back to Spain. (He got parrots, seashells, unusual plants and some Indian people!) On March 15, 1493 he returned to Spain. Cannons boomed, people cheered, and all the church bells rang to welcome Columbus home again!

"There was a big parade to the palace and Columbus gave the Queen gold and masks and pearls and parrots! Columbus was a hero—because he believed he could do something new and he DID it! He was one of the first men to discover the land you and I live in today!"

Let the kids see pictures of early sailing ships and then ask them to use crayons or felt-tip pens to draw pictures of make-believe sea monsters attacking early sailing vessels, or have them draw how the edge of a flat earth might look. If they like the more historic, they could draw Columbus sighting the flock of birds or Columbus giving the Queen gifts from the New World.

NATIONAL POETRY DAY

October 15 is called National Poetry Day because it is the birthday of a poet who lived over 2000 years ago! The Roman poet Virgil was born on this day in 70 BC. He wrote a long story poem, called the Aeneid (i-ne-id). It tells the story of a hero who lived through the Trojan War and after many, many adventures began the family that would build the great city of Rome in Italy.

The poetry that very young children enjoy certainly includes finger rhymes. Here are a few your kids should enjoy.

Five raisin buns in a baker's shop,
(Hold up hand, 5 fingers extended)
Round and fat with sugar on the top.
(Rub and pat the top of your head)
Along came a girl/boy/kid with a nickel one day
(Hold up make-believe coin)
Bought a raisin bun and took it away.
(Hold up hand and bend down little finger)
Four raisin buns in a baker's shop,
(Hold up hand, 4 fingers extended … continue subtracting buns and fingers until rhyme is completed with … Bought the last raisin bun and took it away!)

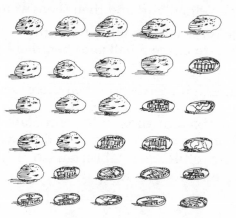

Five little froggies sitting on a well;
One looked up and down he fell.
Froggies jumped high,
Froggies jumped low;
Four little froggies dancing to and fro.
(Hold up five fingers and move/wiggle them to show
actions of the frogs. Continue rhyme with
Four little froggies sitting on a well..." until
the final verse "One little froggy sitting all alone;
he jumped down and then he hopped home.")

Five little pussycats playing near the door;
One ran and hid inside and then there were 4.

Four little pussycats underneath a tree;
One heard a dog bark and then there were 3.

Three little pussycats wonderin' what to do;
One saw a yellow bird and then there were 2.

Two little pussycats layin' in the sun;
One got up to chase a ball and then there was 1.

One little pussycat lookin' for some fun;
He ran after a butterfly and then there were none.

Five- and six-year olds will appreciate hearing story poems read aloud. Your library will have appropriate titles; ask the children's librarian to suggest specific titles available to you on loan.

Here is an epic poem from the turn of the century. (My Mother memorized it when she was six!) It can provide vivid mental images for the attentive listener!

How the Woodpecker Got Its Name
A story from the Northland

Away, away to the Northland,
Where the hours in the day are few
And the nights are so long in winter
That they cannot sleep them through,
They tell a curious story,
I don't believe it's true,
But you may learn a lesson from it
If I tell it now to you.

Once when the good Saint Peter
Lived on this earth below
And went about preaching
Just as he did you know.
He came to the door of a cottage,
In traveling about the earth
Where a little old woman was making cakes
And baking them on the hearth.
Now being faint from hunger,
For the day was almost done,
He asked her from her store of cakes
To give him a single one.
So she took a tiny scrap of dough
And rolled and rolled it flat
And baked it thin as a wafer
But she could not part with that.
Therefore she kneaded another
And still a smaller one
But it looked, when she turned it over
As large as the first had done.
So she said, "The cakes that seem so small
When I eat of them myself

Are yet too large to give away."
So she put it on the shelf.

Now the good Saint Peter grew angry,
For he was hungry and faint,
And surely such a woman
Was enough to provoke a saint.
Then he said, "You are far too selfish
To dwell in the human form
And have both food and shelter
And a fire to keep you warm.
So now you shall do as the birds do
And get your scanty food
By boring and boring and boring
All day in the hard dry wood."
Up she went to the chimney
Never speaking a word
And out of the top flew a Woodpecker
For she was changed to a bird.
She had a scarlet cap on her head
And that was left the same
But all of her clothes were burned
Black as the coal in flame.

Most every little school child,
Has seen her in the wood
Where she lives to this day
Boring and boring for food.

And now little child, remember this,
And try to be kind and good.
You may not be changed to a bird
Though live as selfish as you can.
You will be changed to a *meaner* thing ...
A mean and selfish person.

NATIONAL CHILDREN'S BOOK WEEK

Dates vary, so contact your local reference librarian or The National Book Council (175 Fifth Ave, New York, NY 10010) and inquire as to this year's dates.

Children who grow up handling books and looking at picture books, will find it easy and natural to begin reading books themselves. Kids love to make their own books, so here are some simple-to-make book suggestions. Prepare a variety of these little books ahead of time so that you may have them on hand whenever you need them.

1. Fold several single sheets of newsprint or typing paper in half. Staple together at the fold. The child will outline her/his hand on cover and title this book *All About Me*. Descriptive pictures are drawn or cutout and glued onto the pages. You may print key phrases or sentences on several pages.

2. Fold a piece of colored paper in half and staple blank pages within it. Cut this little book into a simple engaging shape such as a heart, star, cloud, daisy, pumpkin, ghost, cat's head, or sailboat. Child will pick a shape and fill the pages with thoughts and pictures related to that object.

3. Little books may be cut into the simplified shape of a favorite animal. The child illustrates and dictates ideas about *"Why I'd like to be a (Kitty or Horse, etc.)"*

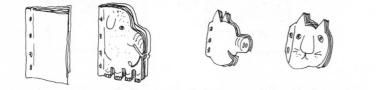

4. Blank-paged books may be used to create personal interpretations of titles, such as; *My Favorite* (Color, Pet, Flower, Holiday, Fairy Tale, People, Animals in the Zoo); *My Collection of* (Beautiful Things, Pressed Leaves, Rubbings I've Made, Dog Pictures, Cars, Tools, Funny Pictures); or *Things that* (Are Red, Go FAST, Are Heavy, Are Pretty, Taste Good, Are Fun to do).

5. Vary the colors, textures of pages, covers of these blank books and let the colors and textures suggest the possible contents of books. For example, make covers of smooth pieces of gift wrapping paper and children fill the pages with pictures of designs and patterned papers.

HALLOWEEN

October 31 is Halloween which means the eve of All Hallows or All Saints' Day. Thousands of years ago there were some people called Druids who believed that spirits lived in trees and certain plants. November 1 was the beginning of their New Year and on October 31, the last night of the old year, they believed the souls of dead people could come back to earth. The Druids built big fires to scare off these spirits. Some people wore costumes and masks to fool them.

Then about 600 years ago in England, groups of "Soulers" would go out on this night, pray and sing church songs, and ask for gifts of money. If you gave the Soulers money, they promised to pray for the souls of people in your family. Today's trick or treating comes from those Soulers of 600 years ago!

Jack-O'Lanterns

If it is possible to take your children to a pumpkin patch or farmer's market to pick out their own pumpkins, *do* it! If this is not feasible, buy 2-3 big pumpkins or a tiny one for each kid. Let them draw faces with felt-tip markers, right onto the pumpkins. Carefully cut exactly on their lines and let them lift off the lids and clean out the pumpkin's insides. Votive candles (in little glass cups) are a quick way to light up each jack-o'lantern.

Halloween Science

Have (encyclopedia) pictures of bats available for the kids to see.

"At Halloween time you'll see a lot of pictures of bats and spiders. Let's learn a little bit about these two animals!

Bats. "Bats can fly but they are not birds. How are bats different from birds? (Bats have hair and sharp teeth while birds have feathers and no teeth. Bat babies are born alive and drink their mother's milk. Birds are hatched from eggs and eat worms and bugs.) Most birds fly in the daylight and sleep at night—just like us. Bats fly after the sun goes down.

"Most bats eat insects—bugs, flies, and moths. Some bats that live in very hot places eat fruit and the pollen from flowers. Some bats eat fish and smaller bats ... Some bats eat blood.

"Blood-eating bats are called vampire bats. They live in very hot places like South America. Their wings are about 12 inches wide and their bodies are about 4 inches long. (Have a ruler handy so that the kids can see these measurements.) They have tiny front teeth that are like needles. They make little cuts with these two teeth into an animal's skin. Then they lap up the blood with their tongues.

"People have felt afraid of bats because they began to think that all bats were blood suckers! But really most bats are quite shy and eat bugs and only fly around when you are in bed asleep."

Spiders. "There are many different kinds of spiders. They have different shapes and colors. Another way you can tell spiders apart is by the kind of webs they spin.

"Garden spiders make round spider webs (see A). House spiders make cobwebs that are kind of like a sheet (see B). Grass spiders, like the wolf spider, make a web shaped like a funnel that goes into a hole in the ground (see C). Dome spiders make a round dome web and then hide under it and wait for their dinner to walk by (see D). The only common poisonous spider we have is the black widow spider. She spins a web made of little pieces of silk that go back and forth any which way (see E).

"The silk that webs are made of is spun out of the body of the spider. It comes out of two little faucets at the

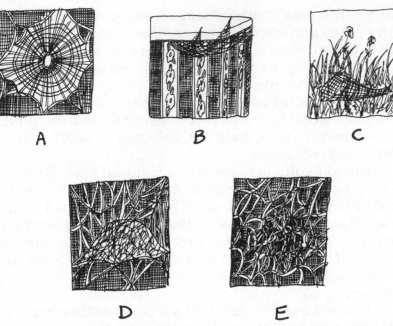

A B C

D E

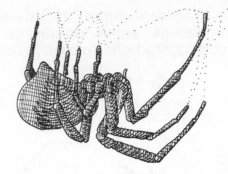

rear of the spider. When the silk comes out at first, it is like water. It gets hard when air hits it. The first threads that the spider spins are used to hold up the web. These threads are smooth, but the inside threads of the web are very sticky. Guess why. (They catch bugs for the spider to eat!) When a bug flies into the sticky part of a spider web, it gets caught and shakes the web. Then OUT comes the spider! The spider spins silk threads round and round the bug, tying it up tight. Then the spider bites the bug with its fangs. It shoots some special stuff into the bug to make the bug's insides get all watery. Now when the spider gets hungry it will go up to the bug and *drink* its dinner. When the spider is finished, the bug's hard outside shell will be all that is left!

"Spiders are really quite shy animals. They will usually run away fast whenever you come near their web!"

Some Halloween Art Projects

1. Cover the windows with a coat of glass wax. Let it dry. Once opaque, the wax is a spooky surface for the children to draw on with their fingers. They'll love making ghosts and jack-o'lanterns and you can eventually clean the windows with a soft dry cloth.

2. Give the kids big pieces of paper and a selection of juicy tempera colors: green, orange, purple, red. Ask them to paint the scariest monsters they can imagine.

3. Older children can brush or dribble rubber cement onto white paper. Ghosts or misty scenes are good subjects. A wash of dark watercolor or tempera paint is applied to the entire sheet of paper. (Pull paper through a pan of diluted water-base paint and call this the Magic Bath.) Once the paint is thoroughly dry, the rubber cement is gently rubbed away, leaving an eerie drawing in relief.

4. On tagboard have each kid draw a big outline of a ghost with eyes and a mouth. Cut out the shape and the features and have the child cover the ghost with a sheet of newsprint. Paper clip the ghost and newsprint together. Have the child use the side of a crayon to rub back and forth across the newsprint. Little by little, their ghost will appear!

5. It's a little messy but a lot of fun: drawing and smudging with charcoal on orange paper! (You can set the chalk and charcoal drawings with a thin coat of hair spray.)

6. Using a little squeeze bottle of glue, each child can draw an outline of a ghost or monster on black paper. Thick white yarn is pressed onto the glue outline to emphasize the spirit's shape. Paper hole-reinforcers are stuck on for the eyes!

Mask-making

Very simple masks are most appropriate for young children. The following one is a good example. Use a medium-sized brown paper bag. Open up the bag and cut it off 4 inches from the bottom, along three sides. Cut the front side in one of several ways, depending on whether the child wants an owl, goblin, cat, or bat outline. Next, the child folds the bag flat and draws in features and adds color to outline. Finished masks are worn on heads (with noses or wings coming down onto foreheads, perhaps). Add to the spirit of the day without making any youngster feel claustrophobic.

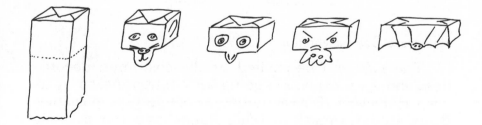

Round ice cream cartons (obtained from an ice cream shop and washed clean) provide the basis for quick masks, including astronauts, clowns, birds, or whatever. Poster-painted features, yarn or raffia hair, and the addition of a hat or beard all add to the variety of forms these cartons may take.

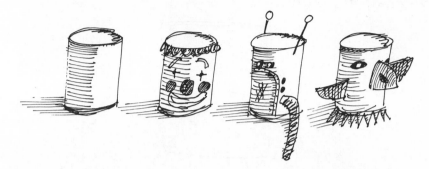

Your five- or six-year olds may enjoy the following mask-making project.

Cut 18 inches of heavy duty cooking aluminum foil. Double the foil in half. Gently press the foil over the child's face and mold it against the eyes, mouth, and nose. Carefully lift the foil off the face. Fold under any excess foil to make mask's outer edge smooth. Use sharp-pointed scissors to cut out eyeholes.

Paper punch a hole at each temple, not too close to the mask's edge. Reinforce holes by gluing a paper hole reinforcer to the inside of each hole. Insert cord and tie to each hole.

Now add liquid dishwashing detergent to tempera paints and let the child paint this life mask in any way he or she likes!

Quick Costumes

Costume jewelry, a long skirt, and a scarf transform a child into a gypsy or a fortuneteller. A black eyepatch, one gold-hoop earring, a scarf on the head, and an eyebrow pencil mustache change any kid into a pirate.

Big plastic garbage bags can also become a costume in five minutes. Cut off the bottom seam of the bag and cut up one side to obtain a flat piece of plastic. If you're using black plastic, you can make a bat costume or a witch-doctor outfit.

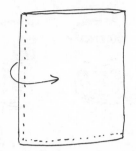

Bat: Measure the length from the child's neck to wrist. Cut out two big bat wings to this length. Use black tape to fasten onto the child at the wrist and neck. Child may wear black clothes and a black mask to complete the costume.

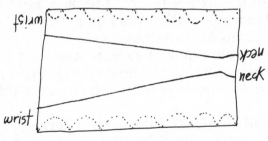

Witch Doctor: Cut the plastic into ½-inch wide strips all along its width. Cut strips to within one inch of the top of the plastic. Gather the top of the plastic around the child's neck so that strips flow down over shoulders and body. The mask is a big brown paper bag with large round eyeholes cut out. The paper bag is painted in poster paint with big bright geometric designs. Raffia hair stapled to the top of the bag completes this costume.

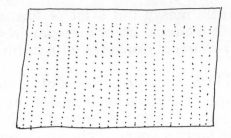

A Hula Girl Skirt can be quickly made by cutting flat green plastic into ½-inch wide strips as suggested for the witch doctor. Gather the bag around the child's waist. Use masking tape to form waistband and to keep skirt up. Cut the length of skirt to fit the child. Leis and bracelets of crepe paper or artificial flowers will add the final touch to this quickie costume. You can also make a pattern for a witch's cape.

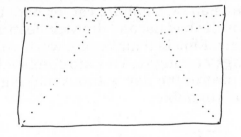

Halloween Day Celebration

The kids will be excited by the costumes, decorations and the prospects of going trick or treating, so try to keep Halloween Day activities as calming as possible. Bring an extra mask (a Lone Ranger type) or a small sheet with eyeholes for the child who may want a costume, but hasn't worn one.

Read the children a Halloween story or two while sitting in their cave (directions are given in "October

Environment") and then help them construct some simple paper puppets and act out the main parts of one of the stories they've just heard. (See "October Puppets")

Perhaps your kids will want to have some active fun. See how they'd enjoy a Halloween game! *Shadows* is begun by having one child, the witch (or warlock), walk around the room. He or she taps a child on the shoulder and says, "*You're* my *shadow.* Come with *me,* Dearee." The child must follow the witch around the room. This routine is repeated until 5 or 6 kids are the witch's shadows. At some point the witch will abruptly stop, clap his or her hands above his or her head and shout, "Run, Shadows, *run!*" at which point the children race to their seats. The first one seated becomes the new witch (or warlock) and the game continues.

For refreshments serve them homemade honey-corn and apple slices or whole wheat donuts and milk.

Homemade Honey-Corn

1 cup honey
½ cup butter
1 tsp vanilla
12 cups popped corn
(2 cups shelled peanuts)

Heat honey and butter till blended. Cool. Mix popped corn and peanuts. Pour honey-butter mixture over popped corn stirring as you pour. Once corn is well coated, spread it in a single layer on a cookie sheet.

Bake at 350° F. for 5-10 minutes until crisp, stirring once or twice. (*Watch corn carefully* as it can burn very quickly!)

OCTOBER SCIENCE

Leaves and Seeds in Autumn

In the fall children may ask, "Why do the leaves change colors?" Leaf coloration is the result of a combination of factors but you may explain it to them in this way: "The green color in plants is called chlorophyll. This green color covers up yellows and reds that are also in the leaves of trees. When it gets cold outside, the chlorophyll, the green in the leaves, goes away. All of a sudden we get to see the yellow and gold and reds that have always been there in the leaves! Coldness makes leaves show their colors. Also how much sunshine and water a tree gets has something to do with how bright a tree's leaves will be.

"Sometimes the leaves on trees growing in a city will not change color. Can you guess why? (The air in a city is often dirty. This dirty air coats the leaves on the trees. It covers the leaves with dirt and grease. This keeps some sunlight and coldness off the leaves and stops them from turning yellow and red in fall.) The brightest leaves will be found on trees growing in fresh air and a cool climate."

Some Fun with Leaves and Seeds

Purchase three rolls of cellophane in yellow, green, and red. Let the kids experiment with overlays of the colors found in leaves, such as green on yellow and green on red. "What color would each of these two leaves appear to be?" This may help them better understand how the leaves appear to change their colors in the fall.

Go on a walk with your kids and collect brightly colored leaves. Press them between layers of newspaper weighted down with several bricks. (Wait until January and bring out these pressed leaves. After the children have enjoyed the fall colors in the midst of winter, you can help them re-constitute the leaves by putting them between moistened paper for a day or two.)

Leaf Prints

Look around your school for an azalea, bayberry, or other bush with overlapping leaves. Check the leaves on the bush to see if they may have some prints on the lower leaves made by the upper leaves casting shadows on them. You will see a print of the upper leaf in yellow or green surrounded by red where sunlight fell directly on the lower leaf.

The children can pin a big leaf to a piece of red construction paper and leave it in direct sunlight for a day. When they bring the paper indoors and remove the leaf, its print should appear on the paper in somewhat the way that the leaves on the bush were printed.

Older children may enjoy this activity. Put a sheet of carbon paper on a table, carbon side up. Put the leaf, vein side down, on top of the carbon paper. Lay a sheet of typing paper over the leaf. Carefully use a warm iron to press the leaf. Remove the sheet of carbon paper. Lay the carboned side of the leaf on top of a piece of fabric (or plastic or vinyl). Press the leaf with a hot iron to transfer the print. Take the fabric outside and spray with Verathane to make the print permanent.

Seeds in Autumn

Go out with the children and help them collect a variety of seeds (milkweed, acorns, maple, cattail, pine cones, cockleburs) and don't forget the weeds and grasses! Bring these seed samples back to school and let the kids group them and try to categorize how they travel. (The milkweed, cattail, and maple are carried by the wind so they fly. The pine cones and acorns are carried off by animals who want to store them, or they fall to the ground; cockleburs and burdock and beggar's ticks catch onto people's clothes or animals' fur and get carried off to new places.)

Seeds come in many sizes and shapes. Help the children list the seeds that we eat (sunflower, sesame, poppy, pumpkin, beans, corn, rice, coffee, peas, caraway, and all the nuts, such as walnuts, peanuts, pecans, and almonds).

Gently open some seeds. Show the kids how the insides of seeds contain the same parts: the baby sprouts (plumule), the baby root (radicle) and the meaty leaf (cotyledon) which will feed the sprout and root until the real leaves can begin to make food for the plant. The outside coat of the seed keeps it from beginning to sprout too early or in the wrong place.

Explain to the children that "a seed needs water in order to break its outside coat. Then the root will grow down and hold onto the earth and start giving the plant water and minerals to live on! This is why a seed cannot grow in water only: it needs food from the ground (and sun) besides the food that it can get from water."

Try sprouting some lemon seeds or beans in water, or on wet cotton balls, so that the children may watch a seed open, sending out the sprout and baby root.

Store the seeds and cones you collect in jars with tight-fitting lids. You can then use the seeds throughout the winter in nature collages, to build pine cone pyramids, or as holiday decorations.

INDOOR FUN WITH SAND

Sandcasting

Help the kids collect many small natural objects, e.g. interesting rocks, shells, gnarled wood pieces, water-smoothed glass, seed pods, and feathers. Other small objects such as buttons, little pieces of broken tile, mirror, marbles, screws, and bolts can also be accumulated.

You will need a half-gallon waxed milk carton for each child and enough sand to fill each carton ¾ full. You'll also need a spray bottle of water for moistening the sand and a small stick or pencil for each child to use for drawing in the wet sand. Toothpicks, spoons, plaster of Paris, water, and a plastic wastebasket will complete your list of needs.

Cut off one side of each milk carton. Fill each carton ¾ full of sand. Let the kids spray their sand to dampen it. Then give each child a stick or pencil and ask that a picture or design be outlined in the sand. Use spoons to scoop out 2-3 inches of sand within their outlines. Spray the sand again. Have them press objects firmly down into the wet sand. Objects may be pressed down and lifted up, leaving impressions. If an object is to be left in the sand sculpture, press it into the sand FACE DOWN.

Mix the plaster in the plastic wastebasket following the directions on package. Use a plastic cup to ladle plaster from the wastebasket and pour it onto freshly moistened sand. Be careful to fill each indentation in the sand. Insert a metal picture hanging hook into the plaster. Ask the child to put the toothpick down into the plaster, and then take it out again. Repeat this again and again all over the plaster's surface. This helps any trapped air bubbles to escape. Let the sandcasts sit overnight without moving them.

The next day, help the kids lift their sand sculptures out of the cartons. Give them soft dry paintbrushes to help them brush off the excess sand from the sculptures' surfaces. Also polish any glass, mirror, plastic, or metal surfaces with a small scrap of cloth. Hang their sandcasts so everyone may enjoy and admire them.

OCTOBER FIELD TRIPS

Fire Prevention Week or any other week this month would be a perfect time to contact your local fire department and inquire if you might bring your kids to see the fire engines and meet a firefighter or two. If possible, arrange to have a firefighter show the children around, clang the bell, slide down the quick-exit pole and, if at *all* possible, climb on the fire engine. The kids should love it!

To celebrate National Children's Book Week, you might visit the children's department of your local library. Call ahead of time and request that a librarian be prepared to read two or three short story books to your group. It's a very good idea for students to hear stories read aloud by a variety of voices and persons.

Inquire by telephone to learn if any of the following would have appropriate personnel to make it possible for your children to visit: a veterinarian who may handle and understand injured wildlife, a farmer who could show the kids what must be done on a farm in order to prepare for winter, or a pet shop owner who could take the time to show the kids various pets and perhaps let them touch a few.

ENRICHMENT OBJECTS

The White Mountain Freezer Company manufactures a wonderful adaptation of the old manual apple peeler. The White Mountain Apple Parer-Corer and Slicer (model 300) does it all in one 5-second operation. Kids just love turning the crank and watching the apple being peeled (and sliced and cored if you wish) right on the spot!

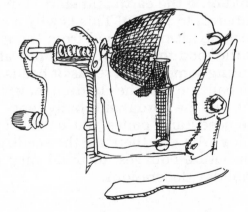

This sturdy machine will last a lifetime and provide hours of intrigue and help in the kitchen. Write and request prices from:

White Mountain Freezer Co.
P.O. Box 231
Winchendon, MA 01475

Consider investing in a hand-held butter churn. Making butter in a churn is far easier than trying to shake a jar of cream until the contents turn to butter. There is something soothing and yet exhilarating about cranking away, watching the paddles churning—and Little Miss Muffet's curds and whey become a reality!

OCTOBER ENVIRONMENT

Make an indoor cave. Contact a large appliance store, arranging to obtain a refrigerator or commercial freezer box (two boxes can be used to make an enormous cave or a cavern).

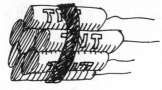

Lay the box on its side. Let the children use brown, black and grey tempera to paint the exterior of the boxes to look earth-covered. Retain the front end flap of the box and fold it to become an open door to the cave. Use long tangles of green and tan crepe paper streamer vines to hang down over the sides and opening of the cave. Pad the inside of the cave with lots of big pillows. Kids will enjoy crawling in and out of their cave.

Here are some other ways they can use it. *As a quiet dim place to sit and have fun with their senses*: Let the children pass each of the following materials one at a time, touch it and say how it makes them feel (or if it ever was alive, and what it may be). Materials might include velvet, sponge, fur, oilcloth, lace, sandpaper, aluminum, cotton, corrugated paper, and corduroy.

As a calm place in which to listen to a story: you start the story and one of them continues it until you go on with it and then again one of them adds a bit and soon...

As a darkened environment in which to really taste the differences between a few unusual flavors, e.g., a piece of fresh coconut, a few pomegranate seeds, a slice of red bell pepper, a sprig of parsley, and a small chunk of dill pickle. Encourage them to use words to describe each flavor, i.e., sweet, salty, sour, tangy, oily, spicey, refreshing.

As a place in which to develop their olfactory discrimination—their sense of smell. Pass to each child a plastic sandwich bag which contains something aromatic. You might saturate small cotton balls with a food flavoring extract: peppermint, maple, anise, brandy, lemon, orange, or a drop of strong coffee, motor oil, liquid detergent, or perfume.

OCTOBER PUPPETS

Take a 12″ × 18″ piece of paper and fold it into thirds lengthwise. Then fold it in half across the middle; leave an open edge on top. Fold the top part back over itself in halves once again and then fold back the bottom part in the opposite direction.

Tape the inside edges of the top part to the inside edges of the bottom part. Be sure you catch the middle fold when you tape. Leave the top and bottom outside

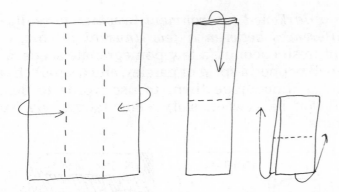

edges open so that there are little openings for the fingers to manipulate the puppet.

Glue a tongue to the inside of the front fold. Also glue on eyes, nose, cheeks, ears, and hair. Hats, mustaches, hair ornaments, eyelashes, brows, and freckles are optional.

These puppets can easily be turned into witches, devils, queens, or pirates for Halloween!

OCTOBER RECIPES

Included here are two recipes that use your jack-o'lanterns after Halloween.

Pumpkin Muffins

(Peel, boil and drain pumpkin to make one cup.)
2¼ cups and 2½ tsp unbleached flour
¾ tsp baking powder
½ tsp salt
½ tsp *each*: cinnamon, ginger, and nutmeg

Sift the dry ingredients together and then add 1¼ cups minus 1 T honey. Cut in: ½ cup minus ½ tsp shortening. Dissolve 1 tsp baking soda in ¾ cup milk. Beat 2 eggs.

Add milk mixture to 2 eggs and then add 1 cup of peeled and boiled pumpkin. (Raisins may also be added.) Let the children add the raisins, honey, and beaten eggs.

Gently combine flour and pumpkin mixtures and spoon into paper cupcake holders inserted into muffin tins. Fill each holder ⅔ full of batter.

Bake 20 minutes at 375° F. Serve with small cups of cold milk.

Pumpkin Pudding

1 pumpkin (2-3 cups cooked and mashed)
¾ tsp salt
1⅔ cups evaporated milk
2 eggs
1 T melted butter
½ cup brown sugar
1½ tsp cinnamon
½ tsp ginger (1 tsp. fresh grated ginger)
½ tsp freshly grated nutmeg

Cut pumpkin in half. Clean out completely. Cut into small pieces. Pare with potato peeler. Place on cookie sheet and cover with foil. Bake at 400° F. for 1 hour. Mash.

Use a large potato masher to beat pumpkin and all other ingredients together. (An electric beater is more efficient if children can watch at a safe distance.) Pour mixture into a buttered 9″ pan. Bake at 400° F. for 45-55 minutes (or until knife inserted in middle of pudding comes out clean).

Homemade Yogurt

Let 4 T of plain yogurt stand covered at room temperature for 3 hours. Then put it in the top of a double boiler with 1 quart of skim or whole milk. Float a cooking thermometer in the milk and heat it directly over flame until it reaches 120° F.

Cool the mixture a bit and set top of double boiler, with thermometer still in it, over hot water. Keep water hot enough so that milk is between 90° and 105°. Continue heating this way for 2-3 hours until mixture thickens. Refrigerate. Serve with molasses and cinnamon or fresh fruit or honey and fruit. Keeps for 2-5 days. (Save 4 T of yogurt as the starter for a new batch!)

Susan Masket's Fruit Butters

Place unpeeled, quartered, cored fruit (e.g., apples, peaches, pears, prunes, cherries) in a kettle. For every 4″ - 6″ of fruit, use 1″ of cider or water. Simmer fruit until tender. Put through food mill, grinder or, as a last resort, colander. Measure quantity obtained. For each quart of sieved cooked fruit, use ½ cup honey, one tsp cloves, and one tsp cinnamon (or ginger).

Turn into large baking pan and place in 300° F. oven for 30 minutes or until butter is desired consistency. Spoon *hot* mixture into sterilized jars and seal.

NOTE: Fruit butters are canned and need sterilized jars.

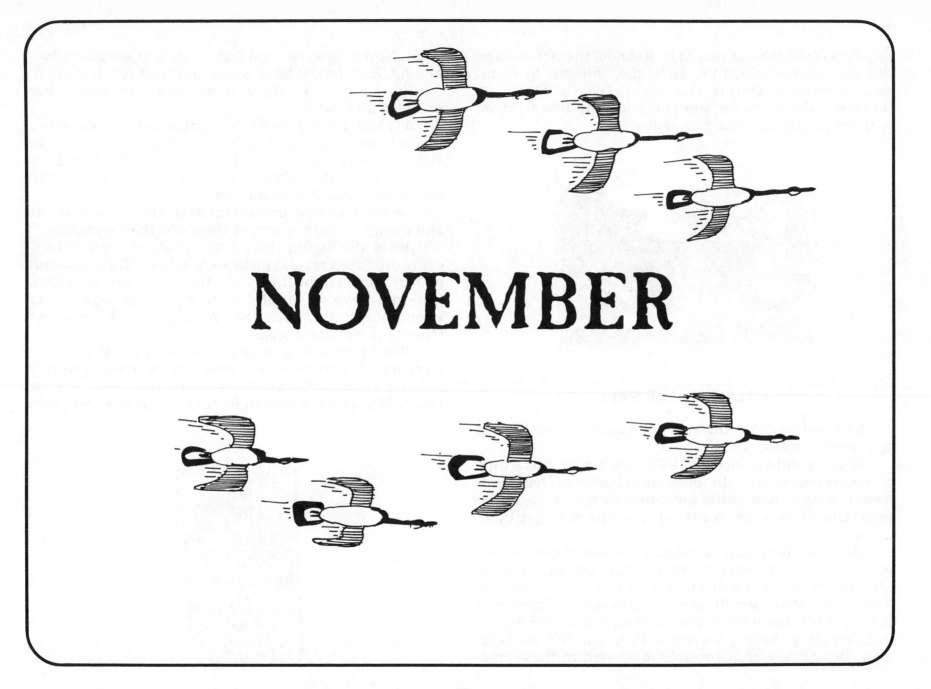

NOVEMBER

This is the time of year to be aware of the riches—and the generosity—of nature. Help the children to count their blessings! During this month of Thanksgiving, think of valid ways for you and your children to share with those who are less fortunate.

AMERICAN ART WEEK

The first week in November is American Art Week. A few words on teaching art:

When a child is involved with making art, it is a time of experimentation with ideas and materials. Over guidance is worse than under guidance. Simply present the materials. Give a few words of motivation to get them started.

See that they can physically handle the materials (work the scissors, squeeze out the right amount of glue); offer quick, pointed assistance, and then let the kids *be*. This allows them the freedom to gain self-confidence in having control over the materials. And it affords them the satisfaction of having created a thing entirely on their own. Be actively and sincerely interested in these crea-

tions. Never censure a subject, even if it seems embarrassing. Kids reflect their world and their reactions to it.

Don't impose a subject unless the child simply has no ideas that day.

A child should never feel pressured to achieve a uniform recognizable drawing. Such pressure leads to standardized expression and stereotypes. Children demonstrate the reality of their minds and emotions, not the reality of physical appearances.

Let the kids have unstructured seating arrangements and plenty of work space, as these aid their creativity.

Avoid displaying trite, cute, outdated, or commercially-produced art and pictures at school. Try to use and display objects and materials that are truly beautiful. Children develop artistic taste by being exposed to strong beautiful images. (See November's "Enrichment Objects" for suggestions.)

When a child is involved with creating, he or she is working on several levels and one of these involves striving to understand this world and how he or she fits into it. It is a very private time. And we must respect this.

Recipe for Fingerpaint (for 20 kids)

Mix ½ box of cornstarch in cold water to make a thin paste. Use a whisk to stir in 3 quarts of boiling water. Cook, stirring constantly to prevent small lumps from forming. (Optional: Add ¼ cup talc for smoothness.) Cool. Add ¼ cup liquid non-detergent soap. Stir until smooth.

Color with dry or wet tempera, or food coloring. Store in a jar to which you've added a few drops of oil of cloves (sold at drugstores); tightly cover. Refrigerate.

Use glossy or glazed paper for making fingerpaintings. Ask your local butcher if you may have, or purchase, some of the glazed-on-one-side paper that is used for wrapping meats.

Roll each child's paper into a tube and submerge it in a plastic pail of water. Place the paper, glossy side up, on a tabletop. Add 1-2 T of fingerpaint to each paper.

Fingerpaintings

Children use their fingers, hands, and forearms to achieve variety of effects. Encourage kids to use a variety of movements. They can also experiment with these paints by using a comb, a bit of sponge, or a notched piece of cardboard.

To remove wrinkles and flatten fingerpaintings once they are dry, press the unpainted side with a hot iron.

Fingerpaint Monoprints

Spoon some fingerpaint directly onto a smooth non-absorbent hard surface, such as a Formica tabletop.

The design should be kept simple, with large colored areas. Thoroughly dampen the drawing paper and press it gently and evenly over the design. Carefully peel the paper off the design.

You will have a single print—a monoprint—that is the mirror image of the child's painting.

THE EARL OF SANDWICH

November 3 is the birthday of the Earl of Sandwich. "Two hundred years ago there was a man named John Montagu. He lived in England in the town of Sandwich and besides being called *Mister* Montagu, he had another title: he was called an Earl. His full name was Mr. John Montagu, the fourth Earl of Sandwich.

Now, John Montagu loved to play card games. He loved to bet money that he could beat everybody else in the game. Well, one time, they say, he played cards all day, and all night and again all DAY. He didn't even stop to sleep or eat. When he finally got hungry he asked the cook to put a piece of meat between two slices of bread—that way he could eat without having to use a fork or spoon! The cook did as John asked and then as a joke, he called the food a SANDWICH! So now you know how we got our very first sandwich!"

Inquire as to the children's favorite sandwiches. Keep track of their answers as these can give insight into their eating habits *and* nutritional needs, perhaps. Ask them: "Do you like mayonnaise on your sandwiches? Lettuce? (Cream) cheese*? What is your favorite jelly? (Do you know the difference between jelly and jam? Jelly is made from the juice of the fruit and it's clear. Jam has crushed fruit right in it.) What kind of meat sandwich do you like best? What is your favorite bread? (A sandwich is more bread than anything else, so it's important to have a good bread on your sandwich. A brown bread is the best because it gives your body more natural vitamins and minerals than a white bread does.)"

Let their answers to the above questions guide you in selecting a recipe. Make some homemade peanut butter, homemade bread, or homemade jelly.

Homemade Peanut Butter

Bring to school a large bag of peanuts in the shell. Let the kids help you shell the peanuts. Put a cupful of peanuts into the blender. Add 1 T of peanut oil to blend butter to the consistency they like.

Homemade Jelly: A Quick Version

Defrost a 12-oz. can of frozen grape juice concentrate. Dissolve a package of unflavored gelatin into the juice. Pour this mixture into a pan and bring to a boil, stirring to dissolve gelatin. Remove from heat and allow to cool. Pour mixture into a wide mouthed jar and refrigerate.**

Homemade Bread: Susan Masket's Quick Whole Wheat (Yield: 2 loaves)

Soften 3 T dry active yeast in 3½-4½ cups warm water and milk (half-water, half-milk) in a large bowl.
Add: 2 T honey
　　 2 tsp salt

½ cup nutritional yeast
　(available at health food stores)
8 cups of whole wheat flour

Blend well. Dough should be slippery and glutenous yet stiff enough to cling to spoon. It shouldn't flatten out and there should be no liquid showing in the bowl. Add more (or less) flour to achieve this texture.

Fill oiled bread pans ⅔ full. Let dough rise 15 minutes (while you are cleaning up) at 85°-90° F., until it increases in height by 25%.

Bake at 400° F. for 15 minutes. Turn down oven to 350° F. and continue baking for 20 minutes more—or until

*Older children can understand that bright orange cheeses have had colors added to them and that such artificial colors aren't good for us. They can also understand that processed cheeses have chemicals added to them. The best foods for our bodies are the simple ones—the ones that are *free* of added chemicals and colorings.

**Another quick-to-make jelly idea: You can produce homemade jelly at school and without the aid of sugar! *Slim Set* is a jelling mix that jells liquids and does not require sugar to do so. If not available at your grocer's, you may obtain it by writing to: A-W Brands, Inc., Carteret, NJ 07008. Directions appear on the package. (You can make jelly completely sugar-free by using unsweetened frozen grape, apple or grape/pear concentrate.)

bread is done. It will sound hollow when tapped on the bottom.
Cool on rack.

When bread is completely cool, cut it with a serrated knife. Help the children prepare their own peanut butter or cream cheese and jelly creations to celebrate the Earl of Sandwich's birthday!

FIRST PUBLIC LIBRARY

The first public library was opened in Philadelphia on November 8 in 1781.

Contact your local library. Arrange a convenient time during school hours when you may bring your group to visit the children's room. Help very young children to select eight or ten storybooks which you can take out and read to them at school. Let them listen to one or two short stories read by the children's librarian while they are at the library.

Older kids can each choose one or two books to bring back and enjoy at school. (Be sure to take out several good picture books that include clear photographs of a turkey!)

ELECTION DAY

The second Tuesday in November is Election Day.

Young children may hear adults referring to the elections being held today and they may ask what an election is. You can tell them that today grown-ups choose who their (new) leaders will be. Each grown-up gets to tell who he or she wants. This is called a vote. Grown-ups use their votes to say who they feel the new leaders should be. All the votes are put together and counted. The person with the most votes wins—she or he is elected—that means chosen to be a leader.

We choose or elect our leaders on Election Day.

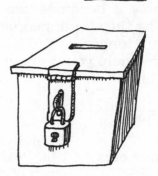

SPLIT PEA SOUP WEEK

The second week in November is Split Pea Soup Week.

Open a package of split peas and show several of the dried legumes to your children. Ask them if they know

what these are. If no one recognizes them, help them to discover the correct identity. Also speak about the shapes. Each split pea is a half; show them a fresh or frozen pea and how it becomes two halves when it is split. Ask them why they think people first dried vegetables. (To keep them longer)

Let the children help you prepare a robust snack for some chilly day this week.

Andersen Split Pea Soup*

2 quarts water	¼ tsp thyme
2 cups dried split peas	1 bay leaf
1 stalk celery, diced	pinch of cayenne or dash
1 large carrot, diced	of tabasco
1 small onion, chopped	salt, pepper to taste
	1 garlic bud, diced

Boil all ingredients together for 20 minutes. Simmer until peas are done (2-4 hours). Purée in blender. Serve hot, garnished with croutons.

(Thanks to Connie Hays)

Split Pea Pictures

Ask the kids to each take a few (5-8) dried split peas. Let them decide how many each wishes to use. Next give each child a small piece of construction paper and say, "Now lay your split peas on your paper in any way you like. Then put a little glue on each split pea and glue it to its place on the paper." When the peas are all secured to the papers, ask the children to draw (or paint) a picture or a design around their split peas. "Make the peas a part of your picture. They could be eyes or flowers or dots or anything *you* like. You're the artist." Display the finished Split Pea Pictures and encourage the kids to talk about them in a positive , non-competitive way. "Which ones do you think are pretty? Funny? Mysterious?" Try to have children say a bit about their own pictures, too.

VETERANS DAY

November 11 is Veterans Day.

"Today we remember the people who have been in the army, navy, air force, and marines—all the people who have been in services to protect our country. We especially remember today all the people who have died in wars fighting to keep America a free land.

"The first great World War ended on this day in 1918 at 11:00 in the morning. Lots of people will be completely still at 11:00 this morning. They will be saying a little prayer for all veterans, hoping that we won't have anymore wars."

You may choose, if your children are older, to have a moment of silence to note November 11.

THANKSGIVING

The fourth Thursday of November is Thanksgiving.

"Three hundred and fifty years ago some people crossed the ocean to our land in a little ship called The Mayflower. It took 60 days to make the trip in those times. (Today we can cross the ocean in a ship in just 5 days.) These people called themselves 'pilgrims' because a pilgrim is a stranger, a person who is not settled down.

"When the Pilgrims landed their ship at Plymouth Rock, it was already close to winter. The men cut down trees and built cabins. The women stayed on The Mayflower and took care of the children. Lots of the Pilgrims

*From *The Portly Padre or Brother Larry in the Kitchen* compiled by Dorothy L. Taugher, page 102, and published by the Cookbook Committee, All Saints' Episcopal Church, Box 1296, Carmel, CA 93921, 1980.

the head Indian chief and his family to a dinner. There were just five Pilgrim women and several Pilgrim girls to do the cooking. It took days. And then NINETY Indians came for dinner. The Indians brought five deer to eat. The Pilgrims had turkeys, geese, ducks, fish, oysters, lobsters, and clams. They had six different kinds of corn dishes, three kinds of breads, and fruits and berries. The Indians brought a new kind of dessert for that Thanksgiving dinner; a deerskin filled with popcorn balls made with maple syrup!

"Many prayers giving thanks were said long ago at that first Thanksgiving!"

"I Am Thankful" Pictures

"Today we have many, many reasons to feel thankful, to be full of thanks. The Pilgrims said many prayers to say 'thank you' to God and to ask that they be safe and healthy all the long winter. Here is a little prayer that asks God to bless—to show good feelings—towards us.

Bless this house at Thanksgiving,
Bless all its rooms and halls,
Bless all the folks who dwell within;
Bless every friend who calls.
Bless every word spoken, bless the food
And bless the roof above,
God bless this house and keep it safe
Within Thy boundless love.

Ask each of your children to make up a short prayer, to say thank you or ask God to bless something; copy these little thoughts onto a long piece of paper that is tacked scroll-like to the wall and read the whole group of prayers

got sick and died. It was not a happy time. But some of the men found some corn that the Indians had hidden for their spring planting and this corn helped keep the Pilgrims alive through that long winter.

"The Pilgrims were really saved by an American Indian who became their friend. His name was Squanto and he helped the Pilgrims a lot. One big thing he did was teach them how to plant corn. The Pilgrims had never eaten corn before they came to this land. Squanto told them to plant when 'oak leaves are as big as a mouse's ears.' He showed them how to catch fish and make a little hill of dirt and then put three fish—with noses touching and tails spread out—in each little hill. They were to put five kernels in each little hill. (Why do you think they put fish in with the seeds?) In late summer, Squanto showed the Pilgrims when to gather in the ripe corn.

"That fall the Pilgrims had seven houses built and a church and three buildings to hold their food for the winter. They had stored up dried meat, corn, beans, squash, wheat, and peas. The Pilgrims were very grateful to God—and to Squanto. They asked him to go and invite aloud. ("Listen to when I come to your part!") The result will be a thoughtful poem of thanksgiving in blank verse.

Sharing with Others

Look in the Yellow Pages of your phone book and contact any of the following: the children's ward of a local hospital, a school for children with special needs, a settlement house, or home for the aged. Ask if your kids might send artwork, homemade cookies, or cards. Then talk this over with your children. Sharing with others is an important part of Thanksgiving.

Thanksgiving Art

Most children today have never seen a live turkey, so they can't be expected to draw or paint personal interpretations of this bird. At best, they will be drawing an impression of a picture they have seen.

If at all possible, arrange to take the kids to a poultry farm that raises turkeys. Next best will be to borrow a bird from a farmer and bring it to school for the day. If neither of these is possible, go to the library and take out some really clear turkey photographs to show the kids how the wings are attached to the body, how many toes a turkey has, how the waddle really looks, and how that wonderful tail is constructed.

Pine Cone Turkeys

These are not anatomically correct, but they're very effective and fun to make (and use later as placecard holders). Large soft burrs may also be used in place of the pine cones.

Bend furry thick yellow pipecleaner(s) around the cone to form the feet. Color and cut out a turkey head and neck and anchor it with glue to the front of the pine cone. Turkey's wings and tail may be made by gluing

little feathers (from a pillow or a chicken yard) to the two sides and back of the pine cone. Older children can cut out little colored paper wings and tail feathers and insert these (with glue) between flanges of the cones. Or they can paint little pieces of typing paper with bands of color and accordion pleat the paper once it is dry. These pleated wings and tail are then glued into the base of pine cone between the flanges. Put final dabbing with glue on edges of the tail and wing feathers and a light dusting of silver glitter and—there you have it—your pine cone turkey gobbler!

Where Does Our Thanksgiving Dinner Come From?

Talk about dinner menus and favorite dishes. Mention how it's important to eat vegetables, milk, grains, and fruit as well as meat. Then elicit from the children answers to "How do we get the foods we've been talking about?" Get kids to come up with less obvious answers, too, such as pineapple fields in Hawaii, gelatine-making plant, refrigerator R.R. cars, roadside stands, wheat fields in Kansas, trucks, etc. Mention the word 'vegetarian' and see if they understand what a vegetarian is—and what a vegetarian may eat this Thanksgiving.

A Thanksgiving Keepsake

Talk with the kids about things we need and use everyday and probably don't even stop to think and feel grateful for. Use their suggestions to make a list of book titles, such as, *My Shoes, Life Without Our Refrigerator, What Is Love?, Why I'm Grateful for My Cat, The Most Important Thing I Own.* Each child will pick a book title and decide on six things to draw (or cut and paste) or say about it. Give them three pieces of typing paper folded in half. They will color, paste on these (and dictate sentences for you to print on some pages). Once pages are finished to their satisfaction, staple them within a brightly colored paper cover. Let them carefully print the title on the cover and their name, and Thanksgiving, 19— at the bottom. Give them white glue and silver glitter to add a glamorous touch to the cover of this keepsake book which will touch parents. If it's saved, it will, in later years, mean a great deal to the child too!

INDIAN HERITAGE DAY

The following is appropriate for older children. November 25* is Indian Heritage Day. "Heritage means those things that were given to us by the people who came before us. The native American Indians have given us many gifts—things you probably didn't even KNOW were gifts from them. They gave us the heritage of these foods: corn, squash, beans, turkey, and chile. They gave us moccasins and toboggans, too! We have certain medicines and beautiful pottery, jewelry, and rugs because of our Indian heritage.

"One of the most important things that we have been given by those early Native Americans is *an idea.* See if you understand it: The earth is like our mother. She feeds us. She gives us things to wear and places to live. Look

around you. Mother Earth gave us our books because paper is made from trees. She gave us our clothes because they are made from plants, or sheep wool, or oil. Our food and houses and cars all come from the earth's gifts. Now the American Indian's idea is also: You should be kind and helpful to anyone who is so good and helpful to you! Let's name some things we can do to say thank you for our Indian Heritage! How can we help Mother Earth? We can be kind to animals and birds—they are part of nature, too. We can be careful not to throw papers and trash on the ground or in streams. We can be sure to turn off lights and turn off running water when we aren't using them. We should take showers if we can instead of a bath in the tub. Showers use *less* water, and water and lights are part of Mother Earth's energy. We don't want to

*Indian Heritage Day may be celebrated on the fourth Friday in September in some states.

make her weak! Always try to be kind to all living things—that's the American Indian idea!"

Try playing a record of authentic tribal music* and have the kids beat hand drums or rhythm instruments in time with it. Show them how to dance in time to the music and do a four count toe-heel step, that is, step down on right toe (1) and lower right heel (2) step down on left toe (3) and lower left heel (4) etc.

NOVEMBER NATURE STUDIES

Sand Projects

Some answers to simple questions about sand:

1. What is sand?
(Sand is broken-down pieces of bigger rocks.)

2. How is sand made?
(When a big rock is worked on by the wind, rain, and the cold, it begins to break down and little pieces fall off. These pieces get worked on by wind or water and they get smaller. The pieces of rock are now sand.)

3. Where can you find sand?
(You can find sand any place where rocks have been out in the weather. A good place to find sand is at a beach. There the water has beaten off pieces of rock and rubbed them back and forth wearing them down. The wind has blown the sand pieces, making them smaller and smoother. Dry stream beds are also good places to find sand. Did you know that some big deserts are really dry sea beds?)

4. Why is sand good?
(Some plants, like the cacti and the watermelon, only grow in sand. Part of your house is made of sand; when you mix sand with cement and water it makes mortar, a thick paste that holds bricks and stones together. If the sand and cement and water are poured out in big spaces, you get concrete. Floors, sidewalks, bridges, and walls can all be made from concrete. The windows in your house and school are made from sand—melted sand makes glass! Sand is also used to keep our water pure, and to make sandpaper, and to fill sandboxes. So that's why sand is good.)

Some Fun (Indoors) with Sand

It may be too cold now for the kids to play outside in a sandbox. If this is the case, you can bring some sand indoors and have fun indoors while learning more about this very common substance.

Straining Sand: Use some different grades of wire mesh and screening to let the kids sift sand. Strain the sand through a coarse screen first. Have them examine each successive sifting. Let them use a magnifying glass to really study the sand grains. ("Why do some sand grains have ragged edges and other bits of sand are

---

*Available from: The Music Division, Library of Congress, Washington, D.C. 20540. Write to request the price list.

smooth? The jagged grains of sand are made from harder rocks than the smooth sand came from.")

Dripping Sand: Fill a big coffee can with a soupy mixture of sand and water. Have the children dip small frozen juice containers into the mixture and take out some of this mixture to use to slowly drip down into a cardboard box. Let the kids experiment with this procedure, holding the juice can higher, then lower and varying the thickness of the sand-water mixture. Tall sand mountains, sand castles, and sand stalagmites can be created and the high sides of the box should help keep the floor clean. ("Why does the sand mixture work best when it's not too runny? Why does it flatten out more when you are pouring it from *high* up? When it falls a short way it hits softer and doesn't spread out a lot. When you hold it high and pour, it falls a long way so it's going *fast* when it hits and this makes it push down and spread out more.")

Shaking Sand: Put a big spoonful of mixed grains of sand into a large jar of water. Screw on the lid. Let a child shake up the contents. Then set the jar on the table so everyone can watch what happens. ("Why do the biggest pieces of sand go to the bottom of the jar first? They are the heaviest, so they fall to the bottom fastest. Why do some pieces of sand float? They are probably little bits of wood or plants or sand that have little air holes.") Notice how as the water clears, the last sand sorts itself out by size: the heaviest sediment falls first and tinier pieces of sand, the silt, finally floats down to rest on the very top of the sand.

Sorting Sand: Actually this might best be titled "Sorting the Magnetite Grains from Sand." Obtain some sand that has a lot of black grains in it. Spread the sand out on a big sheet of paper on a table. Let the kids run a magnet back and forth through the sand. The black sand grains that stick to the magnet are a black iron oxide and are called magnetite.

Now take all the magnetite and place it on a piece of lightweight cardboard. Tell the kids that they can make that black sand move around without touching or blowing on it. Can they guess how? Put the magnet up against the underside of the cardboard and move it around. The black sand follows the magnet! Let the children try it. Finally place the magnet flat under a sheet of paper. Gather up the magnetite and sprinkle it on top of the paper. Watch how the magnetite is attracted to the two ends of the magnet so that it makes an outline of the magnet on the paper!

Lifting Sand: Show the kids a chair, a ruler, a long piece of cord, and a big can of sand. Tell them that a pulley is a simple machine that helps us move things up and down. Show them how to tie one end of the cord to the ruler, drape the cord over the chair back and attach the other end of cord to the can of sand. "If you wind up the cord onto the ruler, you make the pulley lift the can. When you unwind the cord, your pulley lets the can down."

Let the kids each try your pulley and then make some for themselves.

Balancing Sand: Hang a coat hanger over a door knob. Suspend a waxed paper cup by three strings to either end of the hanger. Ask the children to drop a bit of sand into one cup. "What happens? Do you know why?" (Now that cup is heavier so the sand pulls it down.) "How can we balance this scale?" (Put sand in the other cup until the two cups are on the same level.) Let the children experiment with putting sand in a measuring cup and transferring equal amounts into each cup; substitute pebbles for sand; estimate which pile of sand (pebbles) weighs more and then prove it with your scale.

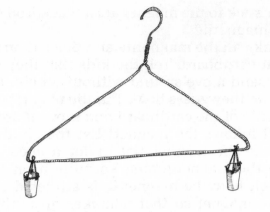

WILDLIFE: HOW ANIMALS GET READY FOR WINTER

"In November many little animals are getting ready for winter. Chipmunks have an underground room where they have saved up lots and lots of nuts and seeds which they can eat all winter long. They also have another underground room for sleeping, and sometimes a third room which is used as their toilet! Chipmunks do sleep more in winter, but they wake up whenever they get hungry!

"Moles live underground most of the time. Their homes have two tunnels, or doorways; one is near the top of the ground and they use this for eating the roots of plants. The second tunnel goes way down deep into the ground. It goes below the earth that gets frozen in winter and this is the tunnel the mole stays in when it is snowing and cold outside.

"Soon after the plants begin to die in the fall, the woodchuck or groundhog plugs up the door to its underground home. It has been fattening itself for weeks now because once it gets cold outside it will go into its burrow and go to sleep. We call this 'hibernating.' Some big animals, like the *bear**, do this also. They will seem to sleep all winter and then when spring comes, a skinny woodchuck and a thin bear will wake up and go looking for a good breakfast.

"Squirrels have two nests: one for summer and one for winter and early spring. Their summer nests are balls of leaves in the crook of a tree's branches. It's easy to see these nests now that trees are losing their leaves. The squirrel's winter nest is made like this. First, it lines a hole in a tree with bark and dried plants. Then it fills the hole in the tree with lots of dried leaves. In the fall squirrels rip apart pine cones and take out the pine nuts. You can see the stripped cones laying on the ground whenever you take a walk in a park or in the woods."

Wildlife Projects

Go through back issues of magazines such as *Natural History, Ranger Rick,* and *National Geographic,* and cut out pictures of animals, birds, and fish. Five- and six-year olds will enjoy helping you find such pictures and

---

*Bears differ from other hibernators in that their temperature, heart rate and breathing do not drop to the levels of true hibernators—and you can awaken bears quite easily in winter: they become fully active within minutes…!

may even be able to tear or cut them out with you. Make sure you have a good selection. Use these pictures for several activities. "There are many different ways you could group these animals. You might group them by their color, the number of feet they have, or if they crawl or fly or swim. You look at these pictures and group them in any way you like." Once the pictures have been grouped, see if you can guess the classification that has been used. Next, you group the pictures and let the students try to guess the classification. This same process can be used with collections of rocks, seashells, feathers, nuts, and leaves.

A TREE BARK WALK

To prepare for this nature walk, explore the area around your school one day during the weekend. Examine the trees in your area so that you may know which ones to use for rubbings, and which to use as examples of trees with bark beetle patterns and woodpecker holes. Use a field guide to help you identify 4-5 different types of trees near your school.

"Remember how each different kind of tree has a different type of leaf? Well, the same thing is true about tree *bark*. Each different kind of tree has a different kind of bark. You can learn to tell the name of a tree even when its leaves are gone. You can learn to know it by its bark! Let's take a walk and collect some interesting bark patterns. We'll make some tree bark rubbings to bring back to school."

Bark Rubbings

Use wide masking tape to tape typing paper to the trunk of smooth-barked tree. Carefully rub across the paper with the flat side of a peeled crayon. Gray birch,

slippery elm, wild cherry, and butternut trees all give good rubbings.

Encourage the kids to close their eyes and *feel* the bark of each tree. If there are loose pieces of bark take them along and later ask the children to close their eyes and feel the difference between the two barks. Try sniffing the barks of different trees. "Can you get to know a tree by its smell?"

Bark Beetle Tunnel Rubbings

Sometimes you may find beautiful hairlike patterns beneath the dried peeling bark on stumps. Female bark beetles lay their eggs under a tree's bark in a long groove known as an egg tunnel. When the beetle eggs hatch, the larvae cut out tiny tunnels away from the central groove and this makes pretty patterns and designs. Oak, spruce, ash, and fruit trees often have bark beetle tunnels in their wood. Kids can make rubbings of these tunnel designs just as they did with the tree bark.

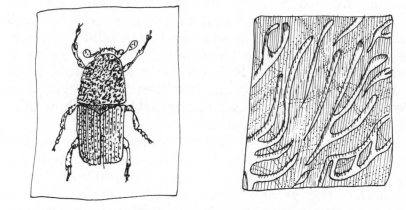

"Woodpecker holes in tree bark often are made when a woodpecker is hunting for a bark beetle. Woodpeckers LOVE to eat bark beetles! Woodpeckers don't eat wood.

They make holes in trees just so they can get at the little bugs living under the bark. Not all woodpeckers eat bugs. If you see neat rows of holes in a tree, that probably means that the yellow-bellied sapsucker woodpecker has been at work there. The sapsucker eats the sap that drips from each hole it hammers into a tree. (There's also a yellow brown woodpecker called a flicker. It has a curved bill and eats ants...)"

When you have returned from your tree bark excursion, try grouping the rubbings into specific tree categories. Pin up a good example of a rubbing of each type of tree bark you saw (and display an actual piece of the tree's bark as well as a photo of each tree type if this is possible).

NOVEMBER FIELD TRIPS

Arrange to take your kids to visit a large kitchen that prepares food for a cafeteria. Plan to have the children visit during a quiet time of day when the cooks are involved in soup preparation, chopping vegetables, and making bread. Encourage the kids to ask pointed, meaningful questions and to be respectful of the objects in someone else's kitchen. Perhaps the children could bring an appetizing or artistic gift that they had prepared in advance for these cooks who have just shared their time and experience with the kids!

If your group enjoys performing for others—singing songs, playing rhythm instruments, dancing, giving a little puppet show—arrange to take them to visit a local rest home. The people at convalescent and rest homes benefit so much by being in touch with youngsters, and children glow with pride at bringing cheer to people who are housebound. This kind of field trip can be repeated at any time of the year—with real enjoyment for all.

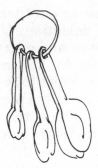

It may be too cold now for you to take your kids on trips outside the school. If this is the case, arrange to have people with special talents come to visit you! Be sure that any visitor remembers to speak using words that little kids can understand and to be prepared for an audience that may have a short attention span, too many questions—or no questions. In most cases a 15-minute visit is quite adequate. Of course, encourage visitors to bring visual aids, objects that kids can HANDLE (and not break) as these always animate the children and enliven a visit. Consider inviting someone from a local plant nursery to tell the kids about plants in winter and to show them a poinsettia up close. Invite a minerologist with rock/fossil samples or a Native American or a rabbi with good short stories to share.

ENRICHMENT OBJECTS

Native American Music Recordings

Many times children learn most about a subject by looking at good photographs or pictures of it. The Museum of the American Indian offers slide kits and postcard sets your children may enjoy. Write and ask for their photography leaflet and/or list of publications for which there are nominal fees.

Heye Foundation
Broadway at 155 Street
New York, NY 10032

Sources of Strong Beautiful Imagery
for Your School Rooms

Museum gift shops are an excellent source. Write, requesting the current catalog and price list. You might mention what you are most interested in: colorful educational posters, large pictures, strong wooden folk art toys, simple games, postcards, inexpensive replicas, reproductions, fossil, shell, or rock collections, whatever your needs are.

Capitol Children's Museum, Public Program
800 3rd Street N.E.
Washington, D.C. 20002

The Metropolitan Museum of Art
Museum Shop
255 Gracie Station
New York, NY 10028

Green Tiger Press
Box 3000
La Jolla, CA 92038

NOVEMBER EATING EXPERIENCE

Have a Thanksgiving feast with foods the Pilgrims had at their Thanksgiving meal. (Apple or berry juice may be served as an authentic early American drink.)

Barley Loaves

This recipe makes 2 small 8″ flat loaves. (Preheat oven to 450° F.)

2 cups barley flour (sold at health food stores)
¾ tsp salt
2 tsp sugar
2 tsp baking powder
1 cup undiluted evaporated milk or light cream
2 T melted butter

Combine dry ingredients. Add milk or cream and butter until a soft dough forms. Divide dough in half. Spoon dough onto oiled cookie sheet. Flour your hands. Pat dough into 8″ × ½″ loaves. Lightly score (DO NOT CUT) each loaf with a sharp knife showing the 8 servings of each loaf. Prick tops of loaves with a fork. Bake for 10 minutes or until lightly browned.

Remove from oven. Cool 5 minutes. Cut into wedges. Serve with butter and eat at once!

Succotash*

4 cups cooked (canned) corn — 2 tsp salt
4 cups cooked (frozen) lima beans — ½ tsp paprika
chopped parsley — 8 T butter

Combine and heat in a double-boiler. Makes 16 servings.

Indian Pudding

Preheat oven to 325° F. Scald 8 cups of milk. Pour milk slowly over ⅔ cup cornmeal. Cook in a double-boiler for 15 minutes. Stir in 1½ cups dark molasses and cook 5 minutes more. Remove from heat. Stir in:

½ cup soft butter
2 tsp freshly grated ginger
2 tsp cinnamon

---

*The word Succotash comes from an American Indian word *misickquatash*, which means "an ear of corn."

1½ tsp salt
2 well-beaten eggs
¾ cup raisins (optional)
3 tsp grated lemon peel (optional)

Pour this batter into 2 well-oiled baking dishes. Pour 1 cup of milk over the batter in each dish. (This makes 2 cups of milk in all.) Bake the pudding for 2 hours. Serve pudding warm with whipped cream. Makes 15 servings.

This is a more elaborate recipe than that given in September. Occasionally it is good for young children to be presented with an experience that is similar to an earlier one they have had. This allows the child to recall, to mentally match a memory with a present experience and to refine his/her ability to compare. "That one was sweeter, softer; this one has little pieces of fruit in it and it wiggles more…"

NOVEMBER ENVIRONMENT

A classroom teepee offers a quiet play area for youngsters. The children should not believe that actual Native American teepees were made this way. Let them look at pictures (in an encyclopedia) of authentic tents made by Plains Indians. Perhaps they will get some ideas from such pictures for decorating their own classroom teepee.

Give the children felt-tip pens or poster paints and let them use these to decorate two old (dry) sheets (which you have dyed tan in a strong bath of coffee or tea). Stretch sheets out flat on a clean floor and hold in place with bricks laid along their edges. Encourage the kids to use Indian symbols as shown in reference books or let them make up their own glyphs.

Lean two 6-foot 2 × 2s in an inverted V shape against a corner of a room. Staple the cloth taut between the

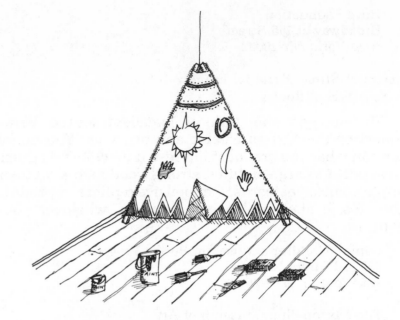

2 × 2s and the walls. You can just fold the teepee back against a wall when the kids are not using it.

Fill the teepee with lots of soft pillows—and remember, of course, this is a place to be quiet, to look at books, and talk together; it is not a safe place for rough and tumble play.

Some of your kids will want to eat in their teepee. Look under "November Recipes" for something they can enjoy inside their warm wigwam.

NOVEMBER GAMES

Pilgrim Father (Mother)

"It," the Pilgrim Mother or Father, stands in front of all the Pilgrim Children who are waiting on a goal line. "It" says, "Come with me to hunt the turkey" and all the kids fall in behind "It" and march around in any direction "It" chooses. When "It" has led the Pilgrim children (far) away from the goal line, "It" shouts "BANG!" The children run back to the goal line. "It" catches as many of them as possible. These kids become "turkeys" and are put in a pretend cage and the game continues.

Each Pilgrim Father/Mother has three turns and then picks a successor from among the remaining Pilgrim children. At this point the Turkeys leave their cage, joining the game again and play continues.

Elbow Tag

Try playing tag on a brisk day outside. Vary the game by designating a certain part of the body (e.g., elbow) as the only place "It" may tag you!

NOVEMBER PUPPETS

Chopstick Puppets

Buy a package of wooden chopsticks in the Oriental foods section of your grocery store (or go to a local Chinese restaurant and ask if you might buy a dozen). Give each child a single chopstick. Have them draw a face on paper which will then be cut out and taped to the

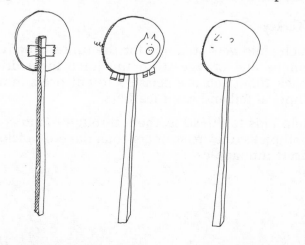

chopstick. Yarn hair can be glued around the face, or a funny hat glued to the head.

Another kind of head can be made by making a ball of Play-Doh, or plasticine clay, and pushing this down on top end of chopstick. Map tack eyes, modelled features, and hair produced by squeezing clay through a garlic press complete this chopstick puppet. Animal heads can be created in this way, too.

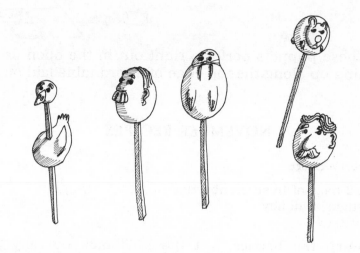

Wooden Spoons Stick Puppets

Keep your eyes open for second-hand wooden spoons sometimes available at your Goodwill or Salvation Army thrift stores. The bowl of the spoon forms the puppet's face and all the child needs to do is add hair, ears, eyeglasses, or a necktie and they're in (show) business!

Encourage your kids to come up with ideas for things they can use to make original stick puppets!

These puppets perform right out in the open or by popping up along the top edge of a card table laid on its side.

NOVEMBER RECIPES

Cranberry Sauce

1-2 bags of fresh cranberries
sugar or honey
water

Wash the berries. Let the kids pick out any blemished berries. Gently dry berries on a towel. Give each child a round cocktail toothpick and ask that he or she prick each cranberry through. This helps the berries cook evenly and keeps the finished sauce from having any sour, unpopped berries in it.

Place berries in pan with water and sugar, e.g., 2 cups berries, 1 cup water, ½ cup sugar. Add only as much sugar as is necessary to sweeten and bring out flavor of tart berries. Cook until berries pop. Cool. Serve small portions with crackers or as an accompaniment to lunch.

Stove Top Cornbread

Butter a 10-inch heavy black skillet. Let the children measure and sift together in a big bowl:

¾ cup unbleached white flour
3 T sugar
3 tsp baking powder
¾ tsp salt

Then add ¾ cup cornmeal. In a second bowl beat 1 egg and then add 3 T bacon drippings and ¾ cup milk to the egg.

Pour the egg mixture into the dry mixture. Give it a few quick strokes with a wooden spoon. Pour batter into oiled skillet. Cover tightly. Place skillet over low heat and cook 20-30 minutes until a toothpick inserted in top comes out clean. Serve hot with butter and honey. Makes 16 slices.

Apple Turkeys

Each child gets an apple for the turkey's body. Peel lemons and oranges (use the juice for a drink at snack time) and use scissors to cut peels into long elliptical tail and wing feathers.

Help kids to thread feathers through round cocktail toothpicks (they're stronger than flat toothpicks) and insert into apples.

Turkey head and feet are drawn and colored on paper that is then cut out, and each is taped to a toothpick which, when inserted into apple, completes the Apple Turkey!

Anchor finished turkeys with small pieces of modeling clay so that they can stand up on a tabletop—until they are eaten!

DECEMBER

NOTE: This is a month in which we adults often over-extend ourselves; children frequently do not get as much rest as they need. The general air of effort and expectation cannot help but affect youngsters. It is wise, therefore, to keep school a calm and soothing place—one of regular routines and with an absence of pressure. Be as well organized as you can be this month—for your own sake, and that of the children.

This is a season of holidays—and one during which you and your kids are going to have lots of fun together!

ADVENT

December 1 is the first day of Advent when Christians around the world celebrate the coming of Christmas. Advent means "coming."

One special way to mark each day of Advent is by introducing an Advent calendar to your (older) children. These calendars have 24 little windows marked 1-24, and each day of Advent a window is opened to show a little surprise, a pretty picture of a Holiday symbol, or a poem. These calendars are placed against the light of a window so that the little pictures seem to shine. Behind the number 24 window is usually found a scene of the Nativity.

You can purchase one of these calendars, which are usually made in Europe, at gift or card shops or you can make one for your children.

A Felt Advent Calendar (to be used each year at the Advent season)

You will need a wooden dowel, gold cord by which to suspend the calendar, light green or white felt, green and red felt, white glitter, scissors, pinking shears, white glue, and enough small golden safety pins and tiny trinkets for each school day of December until the Christmas Holidays (usually 15-18). The trinkets should be lightweight, about an inch long, and can be purchased at Christmas

tree ornament stores or departments. They might include a tiny Santa, elf, angel, and gingerbread child, a little wreath, holly or mistletoe sprig, little holiday balls, icicles, and candy canes. Also include one or two tiny gift-wrapped "packages" which you might make. (Use foil wrapping paper over a little cube of styrofoam.) The final trinket would be a very pretty sparkling star which would be pinned to the top of the tree on the last day of school before vacation.

Use scissors (and light applications of glue) to cut out (and adhere) the tree stand beneath the tree. Use pinking shears to cut the lower edges of the Christmas tree branches. Stitch a seam across the top of the felt backing; insert the dowel and tie gold cord to either end in order to suspend the calendar. The top of the tree stand can have gold braiding attached to it, if you like. Carefully pin half of the trinkets in a line on either side of the tree. (You may neatly write on the felt with the pointed tip of a marker the date of each subsequent ornament if you want to help your older children be aware of each day's date. However, this is not essential to the calendar.) Finally apply a thin coat of white glue to the top edge of each tree branch and

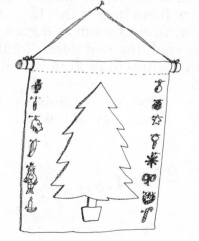

to the top sloping sides of the tree itself, and generously sprinkle clear sparkles of snow/glitter on top of the glue. After a few minutes turn the calendar upside down and gently shake off any excess glitter.

Now, each morning of this month the children may have a quiet moment in which one will unpin the ornament for that day and pick a place on the tree to attach it. Such a procedure has a soothing effect; the children look forward to this little daily ritual and delight in the growing ornamentation of their Advent calendar tree.

ST. NICHOLAS DAY

"St. Nicholas was a real person who was born some 1600 years ago on December 6. He was born in the country we now call Turkey and he was so kind to children all his life that people all around the world got to know about him—and love him for his kindness. He is the patron saint of many groups of people.

travelers and pilgrims

Scholars

School children

Coopers

brewers

poor children

Those who have unjustly lost a lawsuit

Sailors, dock workers, fishermen

"In some places, like Holland and France and Belgium, children celebrate the birthday of St. Nicholas. They believe that he brings little presents during the night and puts the gifts in their shoes so they will find them when they get up in the morning.

"Many stories are told about this kind man who wandered about the land, looking for children he could help. Here is one story:

"Once there was a good but poor man who lived in Holland. He had three daughters. No one would marry his girls because he could not give them dowries, money to get started with in married life. The girls were very, very sad and lonely.

"One night, when the three girls were crying because of their sad lives, the good St. Nicholas was passing by. He overheard their sad story but they did not see him. Quietly he crept up to their house and tossed a bag of gold coins through their window. It landed at the feet of the three daughters and it gave them new lives!"

The people in Holland remember St. Nicholas. Every December 6 little gold-wrapped coin-candies and other sweets are made and shared. Here is a recipe for one particular sweet.

St. Nicholas Day Candies

(You will need a food grinder for this recipe, which makes 40-60 candies.)

1 cup dates (or mixed dry fruit)	3 T orange juice
1 cup seedless raisins	1 cup chopped walnuts
½ cup figs	½ cup orange peel
½ cup dried apricots	shredded coconut

Wash the dried fruit and grind them together with orange peel.

Add walnuts and enough orange juice to help mixture hold together. Stir well.

Roll into little balls. Then roll these balls in shredded coconut. Wrap each ball in a twist of heavy plastic wrap and chill.

THE WINTER SOLSTICE

On December 21 or 22, use a world globe and a light source (a strong flashlight in a darkened room) to show the children how it is that winter solstice occurs. First, have the children locate where we live on the earth. Then explain and show them how at this time of year our earth is a bit tilted away from the sun as it goes around the sun, and so the light from the sun doesn't fall on us as many hours a day now as it will in June when the earth is no longer so tilted.

"This day is called Winter Solstice, the first day of winter. It is the shortest day of the year. From now on—

1 2 3 4 5 6 7 8 9 10 11 12 13 14 15 16 17 18 19 20 21 22 23 24 25 26 27 28 29 30 31

until summer—each day will seem a little longer because the earth will slowly be tilting back toward the sun and we will have sunlight a bit longer each day. You know I said today is the shortest day of the year? Well, that makes tonight the longest night of the whole year, too!"

HANUKKAH

"Some time in December (beginning on the twenty-fifth day of the Hebrew month Kislev), Jewish people celebrate Hanukkah, the Festival of Lights. This holiday is a celebration of religious freedom. Each evening, as the blessing is said, another candle is added to the one lit the evening before, until eight candles burn on the menorah. The ninth candle is called the shamash and is used to light the others.

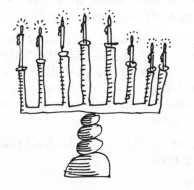

"This tradition reminds the Jews of a miracle that happened over 2000 years ago! The Syrians had attacked the city of Jerusalem. They wanted to kill the Jews who lived there. They went into the Jewish temple and put out the altar light. They made the temple ugly. The Syrians fought hard, but the Jews would not give up. Some Jews had a leader named Judah Macabee and they fought very hard. It took years, but at last the Syrians left Jerusalem and Judah Macabee and his men went into their temple to clean it and make it a good place to worship in again. They wanted to light the altar light to God, but there was only enough oil for the lamp to last one day! And once the lamp is lit you should not ever let it go out! What could they do? Well, they lit the lamp and quickly sent someone to get more oil from a temple far away. The man rushed off, but he could never get back before the altar light burned out…Well, somehow that lamp burned on and on for eight days. Not until the new oil had arrived did the lamp seem to need it! That *was* a miracle!

"Today Jewish people all over the world light the eight candles of the menorah to celebrate their people who would not give up, and the miracle of the lamp that would not burn out!"

(Of course, the way you choose to treat Hanukkah—and all holidays special to specific groups—depends on the ethnic and religious makeup of your children and your community.)

Playing Dreidel

A Hanukkah dreidel is a little top with four sides. Each side has a Hebrew letter: nun (noon), gimmel, shin, hay. These letters are the first in the Hebrew words "Nes gadol haya sham," which means, "A great miracle happened there," referring to the miracle of the temple lamp in Jerusalem.

One way to play with the dreidel is to put some peanuts in the shell in the middle of the table. This is the "pot." The first child spins the dreidel and when it comes to rest, the letter showing tells the child what he or she has earned. Nun = you get nothing; gimmel = you take

nun

shin

he

gimel

the whole pot; hay = you take half of the pot, and shin = you must put one peanut back into the pot.

A Handmade Dreidel

Cut a 2-inch square from light cardboard or poster-board. Divide the square into four sections and print one of the Hebrew letters shown on each section. Use a hole punch to make a hole in the very middle of the square. Insert a short pointed pencil through the hole. Twirl the dreidel to be certain it spins well.

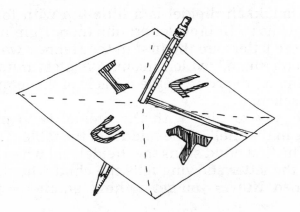

Potato Latkes

Potato latkes (pancakes) are a traditional Jewish dish often served during Hanukkah. You may want to make or serve them to your children.

    2 cups grated raw potatoes
      (measure after draining off water)*
    2 eggs, beaten well
    1 tsp salt
    2 T matzo meal (or flour)
    ¼ tsp baking powder
    1 small onion grated fine (optional)

To save time, grate most of the potatoes ahead of time. Let the children grate enough to feel that they have contributed to the preparation of the recipe.

*Always keep the grated potatoes covered with cold water to prevent discoloration. When you are ready to use them, drain off the water.

Mix the ingredients well. Carefully drop by table-spoonfuls onto a hot, oiled skillet. Flatten each latke a little with the back of the spatula. Fry on both sides until golden. Drain latkes on a paper towel and then cover completely with aluminum foil to keep them warm until served.

Sour cream or apple sauce is traditionally served with potato latkes.

CHRISTMAS

"People have always liked to have holidays in the middle of winter right after Winter Solstice. The days are getting longer again to make people happy so they *feel* like celebrating.

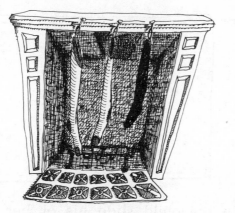

"Christian people have a special reason to celebrate because they believe a very special Baby—Jesus Christ—was born December 25. We try to think of how we can make other people happy at this time of year; that's one way to show we remember the little Baby who was born in a manger 2000 years ago!"

Gift Making

"One way to make other people happy is to show them that you've been thinking of them. When you make a present especially *for* someone—that should really make that person feel good!"

Here are some easy-to-make gifts for your kids to try this year!

A Spindle. Give each child a block of wood that is about 4 inches square. Let the kids sand the wood until it is smooth all over. Next they can draw designs on the blocks using (waterproof) marking pens. Each block should then be given a coat or two of shellac to protect the designs.

Now help the kids find the middle of the underside of each block. "Turn your wood blocks upside down. Use a ruler and draw a line to connect the opposite corners of the block. You will draw a big X. Now right where the two lines cross make a big dot. That's where you will hammer a long nail—right through that dot!" Lay down a thick stack of newspapers. Position the 4″ block of wood on top of two pieces of scrap wood on this newspaper. Now when the child hammers the nail through the elevated 4″ block, the nail will not go into the table. Help each child pound a long nail through each 4″ block of wood until the nailhead is flush with the bottom of the wood block. Turn the block over and there's a spindle!

On a small piece of paper print, "Here is a gift I made for you. It is a spindle. You can use it on your desk or to help you keep track of the bills. I love you." Have the child sign this note and then put it on the nail. (Press cork onto the nail's point before the child wraps this gift.)

Wastebasket. Collect empty round 5-gallon ice cream containers from a local ice cream shop. Get one for each child. In advance, cut a piece of sturdy white or tan paper long enough to go around the can and lap over itself. Cut the paper as wide as the container is high. Cut a paper for each child.

Let the children use poster or finger paints to decorate their papers. Have them fill the papers with color and designs. When the papers are decorated, each will be securely glued (with white glue) to cover a container.

You, rather than the children, may have to do this step, but it will not take too long: spread a thin layer of glue to completely cover an area on can; press paper firmly down and continue until can is completely covered with paper.* Be neat. When glue is dry, give each wastebasket a coat of shellac to further protect the gifts!

Instant Placemats. Have the children make colorful pictures or designs with crayons or felt-tip markers on sheets of 12″ × 18″ paper. Encourage them to get vivid colors by pressing down on crayons or filling in areas with solid fields of color.

Buy enough heavy plastic (storm window covering) from a hardware store so that each child has 1 (or 2) piece(s)** 13″ × 38″. Cut out pieces 13″ × 38″ and fold firmly in half to create a 13″ × 19″ shape. Use nylon thread on your sewing machine and leave a half-inch margin on each side of the placemat as you stitch it, using a somewhat lengthened stitch. Sew across the top of the mat, down the folded side, and across the bottom of mat. Double back at the beginning stitching and on the last 1½″ of stitching to secure the end threads. Leave the left-hand side of plastic open so that the decorative drawing may be inserted there.

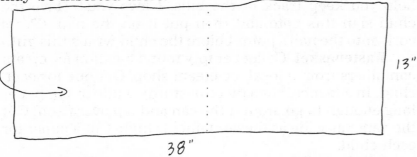

13″

38″

---

*You may prefer to use spray (rubber cement) adhesive: it is not inexpensive-but it's fast!

**Depending on whether you're having the kids make just one mat or one for each parent.

½ inch margin →

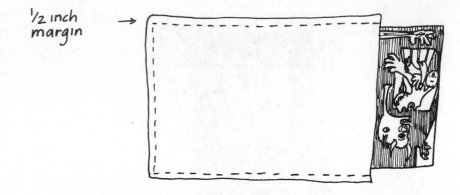

Now help the child slide his or her drawing in between the plastic covers to complete the placemat. The lovely thing about this design is that you can just change the drawing and have a brand new placemat! (Suggest that the child make a new drawing for his or her parent to use with each upcoming holiday.)

Quick Candles. You will need three 1-pound coffee cans, one 5-pound coffee can, paraffin, old crayons, a knife, a hot plate, water, a pot holder, and 1-3 plumber's candles for each child.

Fill the big can with water and set it on the table. Fill each 1-pound coffee can ⅓ full of melted paraffin. **(CAUTION: Working with hot wax is dangerous. Be sure the youngsters do this activity only under teacher supervision.)** Add crayon shavings to each can until the wax is strongly colored: one red, one blue, and one green. Bring these cans to the table. Each child holds a candle by the wick and dips it part way into the hot colored wax. The child repeats this procedure with each of the different colors of wax. Each dipping should submerge the candle to a slightly different level so that a variegated candle is created.

Homemade Mocha Coffee. (Buy ingredients in bulk to save money.) Collect small glass (baby food) jars with tight fitting lids, one jar for each child. (Measurements are for a single gift, so multiply each times the number of children involved.) Help the children mix the ingredients together in a big bowl:

> 2 oz. instant coffee
> ¼ cup cocoa
> ½ tsp cinnamon
> ¼ tsp nutmeg

Help the kids spoon coffee mixture into each little jar and tightly close lid. Let the children decorate the lid with gold paper cut-outs and glitter and tie a pretty bow around each lid. Tape to one end of the ribbon a short note:

Dear Mommy and Daddy,

This is some mocha coffee I made for you. I hope you'll like it. Add 1 tsp or more of my mix to a cup of hot water. You can also add half & half or whipped cream or sugar if you want. I hope you enjoy it.

Happy Holidays!

Love,

—————————

(Let the child sign his or her name on the note.)

Orange Spice Tea. Collect little glass jars with tight-fitting lids, one for each child. Have the children coarsely grate washed (unsprayed) oranges to obtain half a cup of orange peel. Spread this out on paper towels to dry. Let them all have a turn at bruising a quarter cup of cloves in a mortar. Two cups of dried mint leaves are added to the cloves and orange peel. Then let the kids measure 4 cups of black bulk tea and add this to the other ingredients. Stir well and fill little jars with the tea. Tightly close each jar and help the children print on commercial legal seals (available at a stationer's)—*Orange Spice Tea*, and glue one to each jar.

Have the kids wrap their tea in pretty paper tied with ribbons.

(Holiday Note): Ask the parents of your children to save their greeting cards for you. They can be used in a variety of ways.

Kids enjoy cutting out portions of the pictures to use in collages or little picture books.

They can use large darning needles to prick holes all around objects in the pictures; then the card is taped to a window so that light seems to radiate from the pictures, just as it did in Victorian times when this technique originated.

If you cement the card to a piece of lightweight cardboard and punch holes along the edge of an object in the picture, you'll have a hand-made sewing card!

Oriental-Dyed Wrapping Paper

Oriental-dyed paper can be made with sturdy (double thick) paper towels and will be good for wrapping the spindle or candles. You'll need muffin tins, food coloring, water, and heavy paper towels.

Help each kid fold his or her sheet of toweling in any way (lengthwise, crosswise, accordion-pleated, diagonally) until a folded packet is produced. Be certain the paper is folded tightly, however, as the packet can't be over-thick.

Fill each muffin tin with water and a generous amount of food coloring. The kids dip corners or ends of the packets into the dye baths. (Excess moisture is squeezed out between layers of additional toweling.)

The dyed paper is opened up and allowed to dry out a bit; then you may re-dip it in another color. This procedure is repeated until the child feels satisfied with the wrapping paper. Then it is allowed to dry thoroughly before using.

Printed Wrapping Paper

Buy an economy package of green tissue paper. Help the children cut a small simplified star, bell, or tree shape from a styrofoam meat tray. Use white glue and a straight pin to fasten each one to the end of a cork from a wine bottle. When the glue is dry, the child holds the cork and dips the styrofoam shape into thick white poster paint and then stamps it at random over the surface of the tissue paper. A light sprinkling of glitter finishes this gift-wrapping paper.

No-Sew Stockings

Give the children a variety of felt and fake fur scraps to work with. Ask them each to cut out and glue together pieces of felt to make, for example, a little Santa Claus face, a candle, a wreath, a star, or a toy. ("I'm not going to tell you how these little felt pictures will be used; I need them for a little surprise that you'll get on the last day of school before Christmas vacation, all right?") Use pinking shears to cut from red felt two large identical stocking shapes for each child. Apply a 1-inch-wide strip of rubber cement along the inside edge of each stocking— NOT including the top edges. Let the cement dry and

then, making certain that edges match, press stockings together *firmly*! Place the stockings flat under heavy weights (books) for one night. Use white glue to adhere the child's felt decoration to the front of his or her stocking. Add (2-3″) white fake fur trim to the top of the sock. You may also print each child's name in white glue* at the top of the stocking. Sprinkle silver glitter on the wet glue and allow to dry before removing any loose glitter.

Present the finished stockings to the children on the last day of school before vacation so that they may be used at home on Christmas Eve.

You might want to place this gift in each of your students' stockings. Inexpensive and educational, Rainbow Glasses may be ordered well in advance from:

Children's Museum Friends
67 East Kirby
Detroit, MI 48202

Rainbow Glasses will charm your kids...write for a catalog and a price list.

Christmas Tree Ornaments

Here is an opportunity for youngsters to enjoy and benefit from the soothing experience of using needle and thread to make long strings of garland for the Christmas tree.

Have ready in advance a long double thread knotted with a cranberry-anchor for each child to use. Large blunt-ended needles work well. Some garlands can be made from cranberries and popcorn, of course. Here are some other possibilities:

---

*A hand embroidered name is especially fine if you have the inclination and the time to chain stitch each child's name on a stocking.

- cranberries and styrofoam packing (curls or donut shapes)
- small colored paper shapes that have been cut and punched with a hole puncher
- small pasta shapes painted white and sprinkled with glitter
- little stars and moons cut from gold paper and interspersed between cranberries
- plastic drinking straws cut into short lengths and alternated with small colored paper cutouts of circles, squares, stars, and diamonds

Hard Candy Ornaments

Let the kids place hard candies (the kind that have little flower designs in the centers) on a foil-lined cookie sheet. Put them in the oven. Bake for 10 min. at 300° F. (Let the ornaments cool a bit.) Then let each child make a hole with a pencil point in each candy ornament so that it may be hung from the tree.

Macaroni Ornaments

Prepare in advance for each child a 4″ × 4″ piece of lightweight cardboard, such as posterboard, in the shape shown in the illustration.

Give the children white glue and a variety of uncooked pasta: elbows, wheels, small seashells, and spaghetti in 2″ and 4″ lengths.

Ask the children to glue the pasta to cover one side of their cardboard pieces. (When the glue is dried, the back side of the cardboard can also be covered with a pasta design and glued in place.) When all the glue has dried, these ornaments may be painted with poster paints and sprinkled with glitter.

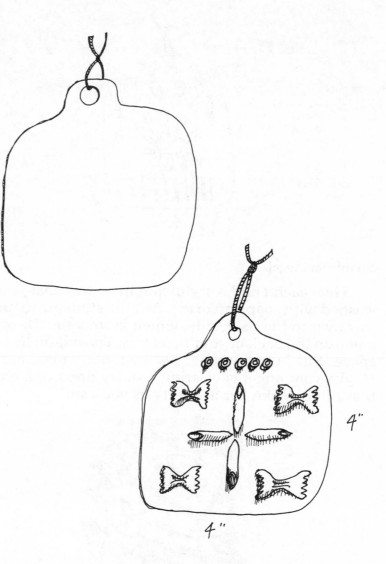

4"

4"

Styrofoam Angels

Give each child a styrofoam meat tray that you have washed with soap and dried. Ask the students to turn the tray over to the back side, which is smooth. "Draw a *big* angel on the back of your meat tray. Try and fill the whole space. Put in everything: her hair, her wings, her halo. Maybe your angel is wearing a starry dress or a crown—that's fine. Make her as pretty as you can."

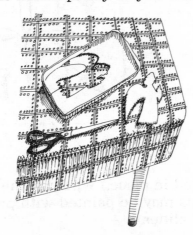

Collect these angels and take them home that night and carefully cut out (using embroidery scissors) each one—staying faithfully on the lines the child has drawn. Take them to school the following morning and return each to its owner. Now the kids can paint their angels with poster paints (which should adhere to styrofoam as any oil should have come off when you washed the trays); add tinsel halos, gold doily collars, and glitter on the wings. Use a needle and yarn or nylon thread to pierce the ornament (near top of angel) and make a big loop, knotting ends of yarn or thread. This loop will be used to hang the angel from your tree—and there should be a wonderful variety of these angels floating through its branches! (Or you can suspend angels from various lengths of nylon thread secured to thumbtacks in the ceiling of one area of your room. The kids will enjoy looking up now and then to find their angels floating overhead.)

Paper Doily Snowflakes

See "Fun-with-Snow Projects" for instructions. Let kids add a touch of white glue and a light coating of glitter to their snowflakes before resting them among the branches of their tree.

Cornstarch Clay Ornaments

Combine 3 cups cornstarch and 6 cups baking soda in a big pan. Add 3¾ cups water. Place over low heat. Stir all the while until mixture has the consistency of mashed potatoes. Remove from heat and cover with a moistened dish towel.

When the pan is cool enough to handle, remove the clay and knead it until smooth.

Cover the tabletop with waxed paper held down by masking tape. Roll out the clay to ¼" thickness. Let the kids cut out shapes using small cookie cutters while you, using a paring knife, cut out a 1½″ × 1¼″ area in the center of each ornament. Make a centered hole through the top of the ornament using the point of a big knitting needle (or unsharpened pencil).

Place the ornaments on a rack to dry overnight.

Let the children use acrylic paint thinned with water to paint their ornaments. Allow to dry. You use a bright colored permanent marking pen to print the date or the year on each ornament. Give each dried ornament a final coat of spray shellac.

When dry, the ornament is threaded with a short length of ribbon or gold cord through the top hole. Knot the ends of the cord to form a loop.

Finally glue a tiny photo of the child (or a colored pencil drawing she or he made of the Nativity scene) to the back of the ornament. These will make fine holiday keepsakes that parents can use on the family tree year after year.

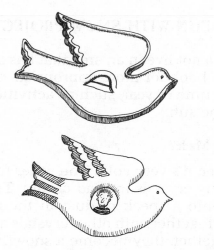

December 31—And so as the old year comes to an end, we prepare to begin anew...

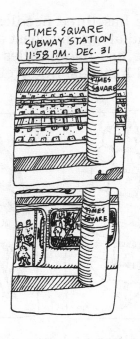

DECEMBER NATURE STUDIES

Plan to take your kids—warmly dressed—on a winter walk about now. As you come to an evergreen tree, ask them to close their eyes and feel the bark and the needles of the tree. Crush some needles and let them inhale the lovely scent. Let them sniff the different barks of evergreen trees. How do scents compare?

Make hot cocoa in advance so that warm drinks await you at the end of your winter walk!

Evergreen Trees

The needles on these evergreen trees are really leaves that have, over many years' time, changed their shape so that they can hold in water all through the winter.

The *Red Pine* has clusters of two needles 6″ long.

The *Pitch Pine* has three needles 3 to 5½″ long. It likes to grow in land along the coast and in sandy soil.

The *White Pine* has five needles 2½ to 5″ long. Its bark is smooth and lustrous. Squirrels love the seeds of its cones!

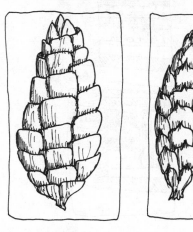

There are five different kinds of *Spruce* and all of them have sharp needles that grow around the twig. And they all smell very pretty!

The *Red Cedar* has needles like scales that grow close together in little groups. Sometimes prickly sharp needles grow on the same Red Cedar tree.

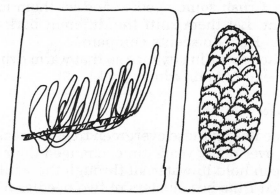

The *Balsam Fir* has a symmetrical shape. Its needles are arranged spirally on its twigs and have no joints or brackets at their bases. Its cones stand up straight on the boughs, giving a candle-like effect.

The *Douglas Fir* has branches from which short needles jut. It is the state tree of Oregon.

FUN-WITH-SNOW PROJECTS

(If you do not live in an area that has snow, check the index of this book for more appropriate projects for you to do at this time of year, such as activities dealing with water, and the sun.)

How Is Snow Made?

"In winter, it's very cold. The water up in the clouds turns into tiny crystals instead of rain. These little crystals fasten onto a speck of dust in the air. Then these crystals join together with other crystals and when lots of them get together, they become a snowflake!

"Did you know that every snowflake is different? No two snowflakes are ever the same!

"When the clouds get filled with these snowflakes, the flakes will begin to fall down out of the clouds and we'll have snow."

Why Are Snowflakes White?

"If snowflakes are made out of frozen water, why aren't they clear like water or an ice cube? A snowflake looks white because its snow crystals have many, many sides and light bounces off the sides and makes us see white. An ice cube, you know, has flat sides so light seems to go through it."

What Can You Do with Snow?

You can magnify it and you can measure it! Here's how:

Magnifying Snowflakes. "Some cold day when you see a soft snowfall outside your window, hurry and put on your coat and cap and then go to your refrigerator and take out the piece of black velvet you put in there *today*! Now put the velvet on top of a pie pan and run outdoors with it. Catch a few small snowflakes. Then get your big magnifying or reading glass and really LOOK at a snowflake up close! Count the sides. Can you find any two that look the same?"

Measuring Snowflakes. You will need a 3-lb. coffee can, a permanent marker, a ruler, and a very snowy day!

Stand the ruler up inside the coffee can and, starting at the bottom of the can, mark off each inch (centimeter) to the top of the can.

Now put on warm clothes and go outside. Put the can out in the middle of a big open area. When the snow stops, run outside and see how many inches (centimeters) of snowfall you have measured!

Paper Doily Snowflakes

Buy round paper doilies of different sizes. Show the kids how to fold the doily in half and then in half again. Show them how to snip out little pieces from each folded side and how to carefully cut out small shapes at the point. Then help them cut a piece down and out of the top of the folded-over doily.

As each doily is unfolded, a unique snowflake (tree or room ornament) appears!

DECEMBER FIELD TRIPS

If it is not too cold you might consider taking your children to visit a Christmas tree farm or a national forest area (where you may pick out your own tree to cut). Contact your local Department of Forestry to learn if there is such an area in your state.

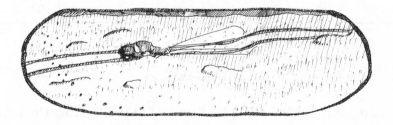

Other December field trip possibilities include: a candle-maker, a doll hospital, a candy kitchen, or an artisan of stained glass windows.

ENRICHMENT OBJECTS

Gold coins "just like St. Nicholas used" are available from:

KTAV Publishing House, Inc.
75 Varick Street
New York, NY 10013

They make pleasant little treats for that last day of school before vacation—as the children sit quietly listening to a holiday story being read aloud.

Hanukkah dreidels (plastic dreidels are very inexpensive) can be purchased from the gift shop of a local Hebrew temple, at a Jewish gift store, or by writing (and requesting a $2 catalog applicable on first order) to the above KTAV address.

Scandinavian waffle/patty irons make lovely lacey cookies that are very festive because they are so unique. Because the cookies require heating oil to 365° F., they are not appropriate for the children to make themselves. But you can make up a batch to bring in as a very special holiday treat for the children or their parents.

The rosette irons are available from:

Williams-Sonoma
Mail Order Department
P.O. Box 7456
San Francisco, CA 94120-7456

In your order, refer to item #313-0026, Rosette Iron.

A DECEMBER HOUSE OF SNOW

For Older Youngsters: After a good snowfall go outside with your kids and take along some bread pans! Help them pack snow into the pans, then gently tap the bottom of each pan to release the snow brick. Set these bricks on the snow, long sides next to each other, to form

a wall … and finally a room. If the workers should lose interest half way through, they will have made a wall which can become a lean-to without much effort.

For Younger Students: Bring a *big* refrigerator box (the kind with wooden reinforcements, if possible) to school and set it on a big piece of plastic out in your play area. Drape another plastic piece (an old shower curtain) over the box. Then wait for it to snow!

Following the snow, go out in the yard and shovel additional snow on the box until it becomes quite covered. Get the kids to help. They'll love it.

One cold afternoon serve the children some warm Cranberry Glögg or Old English Wassail in their Snow House. (NOTE: Wassail means, "be hearty, be healthy." The following wassail recipe dates back to 1870.)

Warm Cranberry Glögg

Warm 6 cups cranberry juice or cranberry-apple juice in a pan over medium heat with 6 whole cloves and 2 cinnamon sticks. When just warm enough to sip comfortably, ladle the liquid into waterproof cups and add 5 raisins to each drink!

Old English Wassail

2 qt. sweet apple cider
  or juice
2 cups orange juice

1 cup lemon juice
1 stick cinnamon
1 tsp cloves or honey

Combine all ingredients in a saucepan and simmer. After several minutes, strain the cloves out of the liquid and serve hot.

DECEMBER PUPPET

Purchase various sizes of styrofoam balls, one for each child. Use a new unsharpened pencil or a wooden dowel to push a hole halfway up through each ball for the child's finger. Cover the ball with a piece of nylon hose of solid colored fabric, and secure loosely with a rubber band at the base of the ball.

Let the children use straight pins to decorate the head with button or bead eyes, sequin nostrils, felt, fur, yarn or fringe hair and eyebrows.

Finally drape a handkerchief-sized piece of cloth over the child's hand. This will be the puppet's clothes. Carefully cut an arm hole on either side of the cloth so that the child's finger and thumb (puppet's arms) can come out. The styrofoam head is pushed down onto the child's first finger and the puppet is ready to perform!

DECEMBER RECIPES

There are so many commercially-made sweets to be eaten at this time of year, that you may welcome a few nutritionally wholesome ones to share with your children.

Carob Balls from Big Sur Hermitage

2 cups honey
4 cups smooth natural peanut butter
1 T vanilla extract (pure)
1 tsp almond extract (pure)
1 tsp coconut extract (pure)
2 cups carob powder
2 cups powdered milk

Mix wet ingredients together. Mix dry ingredients together. Then mix the two together well. Shape into balls and store in a cool place. (You may roll each ball in unsweetened unrefined coconut if you like.)

Sesame Seed Cookies

first layer:
½ cup soft butter
½ cup honey
1¼ cup whole wheat flour
¼ cup soy flour (sold at health food stores)

second layer:

2 eggs
¾ cup brown sugar
1½ tsp vanilla
¼ cup whole wheat flour
¼ tsp baking powder
½ cup shredded unsweetened coconut
⅓ cup sesame seeds

Cream ½ cup honey and ½ cup butter until fluffy. Add 1¼ cups whole wheat flour and ¼ cup soy flour and blend well. Spread out onto a 9″ × 13″ pan and bake at 350° F. for 15 minutes or until just beginning to brown. Cool 5 minutes.

Then beat eggs and beat in sugar and vanilla. Blend in flour, salt, baking powder, coconut, and seeds. Spread evenly over first layer. Return to 350° F. oven for 20 minutes. Cool half an hour before attempting to cut into bars.

Chocolate Granola Candy

6 T margarine	3 cups quick-cooking rolled oats
4 T cocoa	1½ cups flaked coconut
1 cup sugar	1 cup raisins
½ cup milk	¾ cup chopped walnuts

Melt margarine in large saucepan. Stir in cocoa. Add sugar and milk and bring to a rapid boil, stirring often. Boil two minutes. Remove from heat.

Combine rolled oats, coconut, raisins and nuts in a large bowl and pour your chocolate mixture over all. Mix well.

Drop by rounded tablespoons onto waxed paper. Chill and store in tightly-covered container. This recipe makes 24 candies.

Scandinavian Hot Iron Cookies

This is my mother's recipe for 60 cookies.

1 cup pastry flour	1 tsp sugar
⅓ cup evaporated milk	1 tsp salt
½ cup water	1 egg unbeaten
powdered sugar to dust cookies	2 lbs. shortening for frying electric frying pan

Mix milk, water, salt, and egg together. Slowly stir into flour, then beat until smooth. Batter should be as thick as cream.

Heat iron by dipping it into 365° F. oil for about 10 seconds. Remove iron from oil and dip into batter evenly *just up to top of iron*. Dip iron into hot oil. Once batter begins to expand away from iron, use a fork to lift cookie off iron and back into oil. When cookie is lightly browned on one side, turn it over and brown on the second side. Lift cookie out of the oil and drain on a paper towel. Cover with sifted powdered sugar.

JANUARY

May this be a year of joy in learning—for you and your students.

THE 4-DAY CHINESE NEW YEAR

This is a movable feast. Occurring with the second new moon after the winter solstice, it may fall in December or January.

Our word "dragon" comes from the Greek word for "serpent" or "the seeing one." In the Bible "dragon" was used to translate several Hebrew words now understood to mean "serpent" or "Old Sepent" (Satan). The dragon (Satan) is shown in western art as being slain by St. George. In the eastern world, the dragon is a symbol of strength and *good* luck and so it is used traditionally to celebrate the Chinese New Year.

新年快楽

THANKS.
THE
SAME
TO
YOU

It's interesting to older children that all people do not see things as we may and that there are people around the world who may eat other foods, enjoy other games, and celebrate holidays differently from the way *we* do.

Many Chinese believe that the year in which you are born foretells something of the kind of person you will become. Check your records to learn what animal each of your children has as their Chinese New Year Animal.

Horse	Sheep or Goat	Monkey	Rooster	Dog	Pig
1978	1979	1980	1981	1982	1983
1990	1991	1992	1993		

Rat	Ox	Tiger	Rabbit	Dragon	Snake
1984	1985	1986	1987	1988	1989

Prepare a slip of paper with the child's name and year of birth and Chinese animal's name printed on it. Talk with the kids about how each of their animals walk, move, and the sounds it may make. Then sit in a circle and sing "Old MacDonald Had a Farm" and name each of *their* animals as part of the song. For example, "Old MacDonald had a horse (goat, monkey, dog etc.), ee-i-ee-i-o." As their animal is named, each child will move to the center of the circle behaving as if he or she were the Chinese animal counterpart.

In China, the kids receive bright red envelopes today and inside these are luck wishes for this new year! Maybe you would like to fill small red construction paper envelopes with tiny New Year's gifts (sesame candies, or scratch and sniff stickers) and pass these out at the end of school.

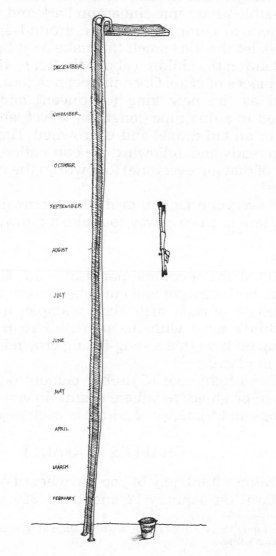

NEW YEAR'S DAY

"This is the first day of our new year. We call our new year 19—. Do you know how many months there are in one year? (That's right, 12.) Today is the first day of the first month! Do you happen to know the name of this month? (January) Well, I bet you don't know how January got it's name! (January is named after the Roman god Janus. He was supposed to have two faces, one that looked back into the past and one that was looking into the future.) Why do you think January was named for that two-faced god, Janus? (This month connects us to the old year and at the same time we are thinking about our new year coming up in the future.)

"Thousands of years ago the Romans would put a picture of Janus over their doorway. This was to say 'goodbye' to the old year and 'hello' to the *new* year. Let's try drawing and coloring big heads of Janus and then we'll put them over *our* doorways to say 'Happy New Year' to everyone who comes in!"

Let the kids create these heads of Janus in anyway they like; every head should be different from the others. When they are completed, tack them all above and around the door to your room. (Add a sign if you like.)

THREE KINGS' DAY

January 6 is the day on which old stories say the three kings brought their gifts of gold, frankincense and myrrh to Baby Jesus. For hundreds of years now people have celebrated Three Kings' Day by baking a very special bean cake. This cake has one bean baked in it and the person who finds the bean in his or her piece of cake is crowned King (or Queen, as the case may be …) of the Bean and everyone must do as the King commands!

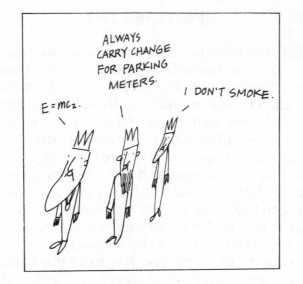

Bean Cake or Kings' Cake

1 cup butter or margarine
¾ cup sugar or honey
¼ cup milk
3 eggs
1½ cup raisins
4 T orange peel, chopped fine
4 T lemon peel, chopped fine
3 cups flour
4 T slivered almonds
1 tsp cinnamon
½ tsp allspice
¼ tsp salt
1 dried lima bean

Cream butter and sugar. Add the eggs, one at a time, and beat well each time. Add milk. Sprinkle a bit of flour over raisins and peels. Sift flour into egg mixture. Add spices. Add raisins, peels, nuts. Drop bean into batter.

Pour into oiled, floured loaf pan and bake 2 hours at 250° F.

Be sure to let the kids smell the orange and lemon peels (they're called ZEST!), the cinnamon, and allspice. If possible have some cinnamon bark and whole allspice for them to compare with the ground spices. And, of course, let the kids smell this cake *as* it bakes.

Caution the children about the bean* that is in one of their pieces of cake. Once the bean is found, the child is hailed as the new king (or queen) and immediately dressed in a fine robe (length of velvet, an adult's cloak, cape or an old drape) and is crowned. Have a sparkling crown ready and, following the coronation, make quite a show of (having everyone) follow(ing) the new monarch's orders!

If everyone feels they'd like a crown to wear, why not? Here is an easy way to make a crown.

Crowns

Cut strips of colored paper 5″ × 18″. Cut a variety of points, both straight and curving like ocean waves along one length of each strip. Have a stapler handy. Encircle the child's head with the prepared strip of paper and overlap ends so that a snug-fitting crown is made. Staple ends in place.

Use a light coat of rubber cement (applied to both areas to be glued) to adhere bright flowers cut from seed catalogs and triangles of glitter to each bejeweled crown!

CHARLES PERRAULT

"I don't think any of you have heard of this man. He was born on January 12 and lived 350 years ago in a

---

*You may think it best to use a whole almond in place of the traditional bean. That's fine.

country called France. This was long before TV or movies and people used to have fun by listening to or telling each other stories! Charles Perrault spent his life collecting stories from all the old men and women story-tellers. He put a lot of these stories together in a book called *Tales of Mother Goose! Now* you know why we still remember this man! He collected and saved for you and me these stories: *Cinderella, Sleeping Beauty, Little Red Riding Hood, Tom Thumb, Puss in Boots* … and many, many others!"

After hearing one of these fine old tales, the children will have fun drawing or painting their favorite part. Collect these paintings into a story book and let them read their pictures with you as they re-tell the tale in their own words.

Collect dress-up clothes and simple props and help them organize a play based on the better-known Perrault tales, such as, *Little Red Riding Hood* or *Cinderella.*

STEPHEN FOSTER

"Today we remember a man who wrote 200 songs while he was alive! 200! And some of these are songs you'll enjoy (learning,) singing. Stephen Foster, born January 13, wrote *Oh! Susanna! Let's* try singing it together."

It rained all night the day I left,
The weather, it was dry
The sun, so hot, I froze to death,
Susanna, don't you cry.
Oh, Susanna, oh don't you cry for me.
I'm bound for Lousiana with my banjo on my knee.

(Other Foster songs include *Swanee River, Camp-town Races, My Old Kentucky Home, Old Folks at Home,* and *Beautiful Dreamer.*)

MARTIN LUTHER KING, JR.

"Born on January 15, Martin Luther King, Jr., was a black American. He didn't believe in using force to get what a person wants. He spent his life trying to help all the American people to be fairly treated. He worked to make this a better world. We remember one of the speeches he gave to a BIG crowd of people. He said that he had a dream that one day all the people in America would love each other and be friends together.

"We all hope for the day when Martin Luther King's dream comes true."

Speak briefly with the kids about using force to get what is wanted. Ask them for suggestions of other ways you can try to get your way. Just get them to think about this idea of non-violence. Plant a seed in their minds today.

NATIONAL NOTHING DAY

January 16 is National Nothing Day. Just for the fun of it, ask the kids to tell you what "zero" means; then ask them to tell you about "nothing." What *is* nothing, or what does nothing *mean*? (If their answers are charming, jot them down verbatim and post them for their parents to enjoy too!)

A.A. MILNE

"Have you heard stories of Winnie the Pooh and Tigger and Eeyore and Christopher Robin? Well, January 18 is the birthday of the man who wrote the Pooh Bear stories! His name was Alan Alexander Milne and the boy Christopher Robin was really his son!

"Do you know what Winnie the Pooh loves to eat? Honey! That's right. Lots of times Christopher Robin has enjoyed tea parties with Pooh and his friends. Why don't we make some honey graham crackers and have a Pooh Bear Tea Party to celebrate Mr. Milne's birthday?"

Honey Graham Crackers

½ cup butter at room temperature	½ tsp salt
⅓ cup brown sugar	½ tsp baking powder
⅓ cup honey	½ tsp cinnamon
2¾ cup graham flour	½ cup (minus 1 T) water

Cream butter, sugar, and honey. Mix the rest of the ingredients together and add to butter mixture; alternate with water. Mix well and then let it stand for 30 minutes.

Flour a tabletop and roll out dough to ⅛" thickness. Cut into 2" squares, using a serrated knife. Place crackers on oiled cookie sheet. Bake for 20 minutes in a 350° F. oven. This recipe makes 3 dozen crackers.

Serve these honey grahams with cold milk or warm berry tea and read a Pooh story aloud to the children as they are enjoying their tea party!

WOLFGANG AMADEUS MOZART

"Mozart's father played the violin. And so there were musical instruments in his house when Mozart was born on January 27 and while he was growing up. When he was 3 years old, Mozart began to teach himself to play the piano of that time (it was called the clavier)! By the time he was five, Mozart was writing simple little songs!

"Mozart had a sister who was a little older than he and together they travelled all over playing music for kings and queens and emperors!

"All his life, Mozart wrote songs and music for people to play and sing. This all happened 200 years ago, but we can listen to his music TODAY!

"Let's listen to some music written by Mozart.* You can paint or use wet chalk while his music plays. See how you like it."

Be certain that all the art materials are organized and that the children have everything they need to work as the music is begun. Mozart's music is best if heard in a room free of distraction, where children are intent on developing their paintings, content to have this music fill their room and minds.

LEWIS CARROLL

"Charles Dodgson was born on January 27 about a hundred years ago. His father was a minister. When he was little he didn't have many friends to play with, so he made pets out of the snails and toads in the garden. He watched them and talked to them and made up adventures for them to all have together.

"When he grew up, this man wrote stories about very wierd animals—and people. He used a made-up name for himself. It was Lewis Carroll. He was famous; everybody read his books, even the Queen of England. Maybe you've heard of *Alice in Wonderland*? That is one of his books! He also wrote *Through the Looking Glass*—another story about Alice's adventures. Both of these stories were written for a little friend of his—a young girl named Alice!"

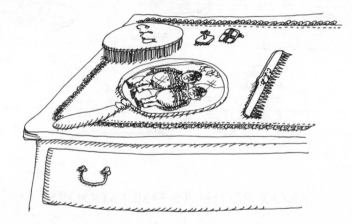

Here is a list of words Carroll invented. Ask 2-3 children to paint a creature to go with each word and then make an Exhibition of Lewis Carroll Word Creatures: snark, jabberwok, jubjub bird, wabe, baragroves, momrath, bandersnatch, and slithy toves!

---

*Try some sonatas for violin and piano, i.e., Sonata in G, K. 301 or Sonata in F, K. 376 or Sonata in B flat, K454.

COMMON SENSE DAY

This special day speaks for itself! Common Sense Day occurs on January 29.

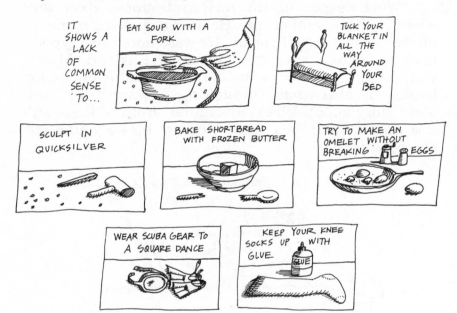

SNOW PROJECTS FOR INDOORS

Snowy Pictures

Cut large sponges into small squares, circles, and rectangles. Give each child dark blue, purple, or grey 12″ × 18″ pieces of construction paper, a shallow container of white tempera paint, and a black or purple crayon. Let the children select 2-3 little sponge shapes.

Encourage them to lightly press the sponge into paint and then tap-tap it onto the papers to create SNOW-falls, funny snowmen, towns, animals, or trees under a blanket of white. Have the kids experiment with overlapping smearing and using different amounts of pressure. Once the paint is dry, crayon is used to highlight or clarify figures.

Snow (Art) Project

"Snow in a bottle" will span three days. Collect one small glass jar with screw-on lid for each child. Help the kids make little snowmen or doll figures by adhering wooden spools, buttons, beads, and little wood scraps together using non-water base glue. Be sure to use glue that is *not* water-soluble. Next, cement each figure to the inside of a jar lid. Let these dry overnight.

On the following day fill each jar, nearly to the top, with water. Put a teaspoon of moth flakes into the water. Now squeeze the glue inside the lid along the edges where it screws on and screw the lid to the jar very tightly. Let the glue dry overnight.

Finally give each jar to its owner and let the kids shake them up and watch while it "snows in a bottle."

Make-Believe Snow

Let the children use hand-powered egg beaters to whip up a mixture of one cup instant powdered starch plus one cup Ivory soap powder plus two cups of water.

They will have lots of fun "painting" snow pictures by putting this mixture on big sheets of blue paper, butcher paper, or even newspaper.

Remind the students that they can't eat *this* snow!

Sparkling Salt Clay

Thin one cup cornstarch in cold water until it is as thick as gravy. Boil two cups of ice cream-making salt* in

---

*Regular salt also works, but ice cream-making salt gives clay its sparkle.

one cup of water. Add the cornstarch mixture to the boiling salt water, stirring constantly to avoid lumping. Cook until mixture forms a large mass. Turn out onto wax paper and cool.

Divide the clay into several parts and add food coloring. If clay sticks to you, wet your hands (a bit of bleach on a cotton swab will remove any food coloring stains to your hands). Place each colored clay in a tightly sealed plastic bag. Refrigerate this clay and it will last for weeks.

Encourage the kids to model snow scenes with this clay untinted: tiny snow rabbits, bears, mountains, igloos. Assemble all of the figures together around (or atop) a large unframed mirror laid flat on a table. Help the kids complete their winter scene with twig trees and moss areas.

SNOW PROJECTS FOR OUTDOORS

Recipes for Snow Ice Cream

Why not try all of these recipes during the next winter months? And then see which one the kids like best. It will be a hard decision.

Snow Ice Cream #1: Of course, always use *fresh clean* snow. Help the kids collect a lot of it in a large bowl. Then bring it back inside.

1 cup rich milk (or even ½ and ½)
1 egg, well-beaten
½ cup sugar (superfine works best)
2 tsp vanilla

Mix the above ingredients together well and then let the kids add the snow. Keep adding until mixture has absorbed a lot of snow. Spoon the ice cream into little paper cups. Enjoy it!

Snow Ice Cream #2: Collect clean new snow in bowls. Dribble sweetened evaporated milk over the snow. Let the kids stir it up before eating.

Snow Ice Cream #3: Dribble thawed juice concentrate all over a dish of snow. Mix and eat.

Snow Ice Cream #4: Dribble maple syrup over a dish of snow! Or economize and make a homemade syrup; have it on hand in the refrigerator for the next snowy day!

Bring 1 cup of water to a boil. Lower heat and stir in 2½ cups (light golden) brown sugar. Stir to dissolve sugar. Add 2 teaspoons natural maple flavoring. Remove syrup from heat (and add ½ cup corn syrup to thicken syrup). This recipe makes 2 cups.

A GIFT FOR SNOWBOUND BIRDS

A Birdfeeder

You will need a 1-lb. coffee can with a plastic lid, 3 pieces of 20″ long string, an aluminum (frozen) pie pan, airplane glue, a can opener, and wild birdseed and shelled peanuts.

Punch and make 3 holes near the top of the can, an equal distance apart from each other. Knot each string and thread it through a hole. (The knot will be on the inside of the can so that it can't pull out.)

Using the can opener, make 4 holes at the bottom of the can. Glue the aluminum pie pan securely to the center of the pie pan. Allow glue to dry.

Fill the feeder with birdseed and replace the plastic lid. Hang the feeder in such a way that children can see and enjoy it (and yet a cat will not be able to reach).

Chickadees, nuthatches, goldfinches, and tufted titmice enjoy hanging birdfeeders.

If you hang suet and peanut butter balls mixed with seeds, you can expect to please woodpeckers. Juncos, sparrows, and mourning doves love cracked corn and millet on or close to the ground.

A CLASSROOM SUBMARINE

Inclement January weather often keeps children indoors. Here is an idea for an indoor play structure to capture their attention and imaginations.

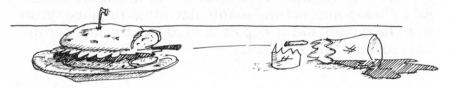

You will need four cardboard boxes for each sub*: one large enough to sit in and three that are somewhat smaller than it but all the same size. You'll also need a cardboard box for scrap pieces, masking tape, a felt-tip pen, scissors and/or a knife for cutting into the boxes, and a big piece of heavy wrapping paper. (Finally, you can paint the sub with any indoor latex wall paint. Perhaps the kids will add waves and fish to the sides. A string of flags and a painted identification number will complete your submarine.)

How to Make the Sub

Stand the large carton (B) on end. This is the conning tower. Lay two boxes (C and D) down in front of it and one box (A) behind it. Tape down the flaps of the front two boxes and of the conning tower.

*This idea appeared in part in the 1964 edition of Child Craft, Field Enterprises Educational Corp, Chicago, Ill.

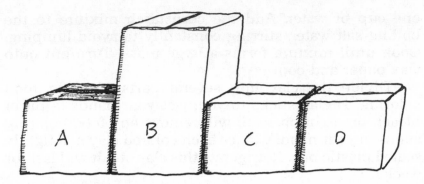

Now you need to make an entrance into the conning tower. Press box A up against box B. Make a line along

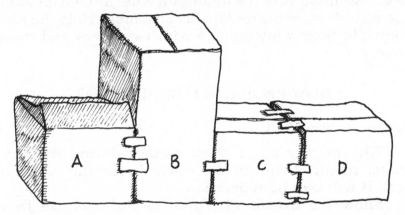

the edge where A touches B. This is the height of the entrance. Cut out that lower part of box B to make the doorway. Keep the cardboard piece you cut out.

Open the top flaps of box A: this is the hatch. Now cut out the end of box A where it meets box B, making a passageway from the hatch into the tower. Save this cut out cardboard also.

Tape the boxes in place one next to the other. You can paint the sub and suspend a string of flags from the tower to the prow and let the children play with it right now or you can (if you have the energy and inclination) continue working further, adding a nose, tail, and periscope to your submarine.

Nose (Prow): Draw a flange-like shape on one of the pieces of cardboard that you cut off box B or A.

Cut it out. Trace around this shape on the other piece of cardboard. Cut it out. (Repeat this on cardboard scraps until you have 8 flange shapes in all.) Tape four pieces to the front for a bow. Tape the points together.

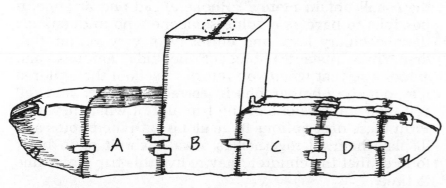

Stern: Now tape four pieces together at the back of box A to make the bow. Cover the bow and stern with heavy paper.

Give your sub a good coat of paint.

The Periscope: You'll need a long aluminum foil box, a little piece of paper, a piece of thin cardboard, masking tape, scissors or razor blade, and two small pocket mirrors.

(Mark the end of the foil box with an X: this will be the top.) Trace a square exactly the size of the end of the box. Cut out this square. Fold it crosswise to form a triangle.

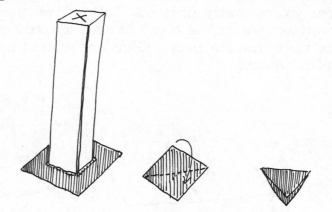

Now stand the box up with the X at the top. Place the triangle paper along the bottom edge of the box, with half of the triangle slanting upwards. Trace a line along the edge of the slant and cut a slit along that line.

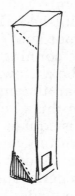

Around the corner from the slit and low down near the bottom, cut a window large enough to look through. Now place the triangle paper at the top of the box on the same side as the lower slit with the folded side slanting down. Trace a line along the slant edge and cut a slit along this line. Around the corner from the top slit (on the side opposite the bottom window) cut a top window.

Now, you're nearly finished. Cut out two pieces of cardboard as wide as the box and a bit longer than the slant of your triangle paper. Glue one mirror to each piece of cardboard.

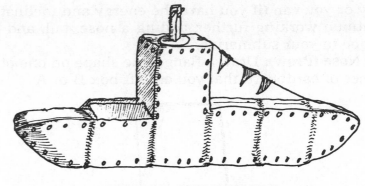

JANUARY FIELD TRIPS

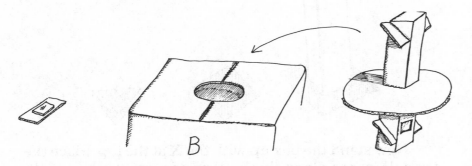

Slide a mirror (with the looking glass upwards) into the lower slit. Slide the other mirror in the top slit (this time, looking glass down).

Your periscope is finished. Here's how to mount it in the conning tower of your sub.

In the center of the conning tower, cut a circle a bit bigger than your foil box. Now, from cardboard, cut a circle a little bigger than the one in the conning tower. Stand the periscope on this circle and draw around the square box. Cut out this square.

Remove one mirror from your periscope and slip the periscope into its circle. Mount. Replace the mirror.

Put one end of your periscope through the hole in the tower with the mount outside the box.

Let the children paint a control panel (with spool knobs glued on it) inside the conning tower. Let them design and make an anchor, too!

In honor of Albert Schweitzer's birthday, you may want to take your children to visit a zoo or a natural history museum. (The inscription at the entrance to Schweitzer's hospital is: "Blessed are the merciful, for they shall obtain mercy.") Phone ahead and arrange, if possible, to have as a guide someone who understands the vocabulary level and curiosity of very young children. Take instant photos of the kids, animals, and exhibits so that when you return to school the children may put the photographs in correct sequence and tell you their impressions of the trip and of what they saw. Print these descriptions to go along with the photos and display them all together as a wall exhibit or in book form so that the children may re-live this trip from time to time.

Heureux les mi-
séricordieux, car
ils obtiendront
miséricorde

Another January excursion might be made to a glass-blower. This can be a very dramatic experience for all of you.

ENRICHMENT OBJECTS

The children can have fun by altering their perceptions (as were those of Alice changed when she went through the Looking Glass) by playing with any of the following.

A really interesting kaleidoscope is available from:

The Museum Store
The Art Institute of Chicago
Michigan Avenue at Adams Street
Chicago, IL 60603

Dover Press offers unusual books at reasonable prices. The children may enjoy *The Moving Picture Book*, with plastic overlays that make the illustration seem to move. Write for a free catalog and check the many other children's books that Dover Press publishes.

Dover Publications, Inc.
Dept. G I
18 Varick Street
New York, NY 10014

An interesting reproduction of a turn-of-the-century book is available from B. Shackman and Co. This unusual little book has drawings in red and in green, one atop the other. The heavy red plastic and green plastic squares that come with this book are placed one at a time over the drawings and make just one picture appear. Two stories appear simultaneously and are old favorites: *The Three Bears* and *Tabby and the Four Kittens: Magic Color Twin Story Book* (#A1561). Kids love the magic of these books and are happy to use the squares and to hear the tales over and over again. Write, requesting a catalog, to:

B. Shackman and Co.
85 Fifth Avenue at 16th Street
New York, NY 10003

JANUARY PUPPET

Give each child a paper cup. Explain how this cup will be their puppet's head. They can paint or use felt-tip pens to draw on the features. Yarn hair and Amish-like beards can be attached with glue. Funny paper ears or noses can be added. A stiff paper hat brim can be slipped over the bottom of the cup, adding another dimension to a puppet. Turn cup right side up and trace the bottom with pencil on stiff paper. Then turn the cup upside down and cover the pencil outline; trace the top of the cup. Remove the cup. Cut a circle that is between two penciled circles: this will fit down over the cup's base. Cut another circle about an inch further out from first producing a paper donut: this is the puppet's hat brim! Paint the top of the puppet's head to match the color of hat brim and become the crown of the hat. The child then slips his or her hand in the cup and brings the puppet to life!

Variations are possible by cutting small finger holes on the cup for a nose to protrude and wiggle around. Some children can even manipulate two fingers (with pupils' drawn-on finger tips) through two cut-out eye holes for a rather bizarre effect.

JANUARY RECIPES

Let's try some new snacks for this new year!

Fried Cornmeal Mush

4½ cups water
½ cup cornmeal
1 tsp salt
3 T flour
1½ cups cold milk

Bring the 4½ cups water to a boil. Mix together the cornmeal, salt, and flour. Add the cold milk to the flour mixture to form a paste. Immediately stir paste into boiling water and *stir* constantly so mush doesn't form lumps or stick to the pan. Bring to boil, lower heat and simmer 10 minutes. Pour into an oiled bread pan. Refrigerate overnight.

At school the next day, turn pan over and gently remove the loaf of mush. Slice into ½ inch slices. Dip each in melted butter and fry until golden brown on each side. Serve with butter, syrup or jelly or honey. Mush served in this way was very popular with early pioneers in America.

Whole Wheat Sticks

1 cup whole wheat flour   ½ cup whipping cream
2 T butter   ½ tsp salt
                            sesame seeds

Cut the butter into the flour. Make little wells in the mixture and add small amounts of cream until dough is formed by pinching mixture together. (Dough should hold together without being sticky.)

Take a small amount and roll this between the palms of your hands. Roll in sesame seeds. Make sticks that are about ½ inch round and 3-4 inches long. Lay on a cookie sheet and don't allow sticks to touch one another.

Bake at 450° F. for 30 minutes or until nice and brown.

When cool enough to handle, sticks are eaten plain or kids can dip them in Honey Whiz after each bite!

Honey Whiz

Mix honey and softened butter together. Whiz it round and round in a bowl until it is good and creamy.

Hoppin' John

(If served on New Year's Day this dish is supposed to insure a year of good fortune to all who dine upon it.)

1 lb. black-eyed peas   2 T corn oil
2 qts. boiling water   salt, pepper
1 onion finely chopped   1 cup raw rice cooked
                            (crushed red pepper)

Wash the black-eyed peas. Cover with water and boil 2 minutes. Then let them stand in the water for an hour or longer. Drain peas well.

Now put peas in a big pot. Pour on boiling water, onion, oil, and seasonings. (Kids often do not care for hot peppers, so use your judgment when adding the traditional crushed red pepper.) Simmer, covered for 2 hours or until peas are soft. Add water as peas cook, if necessary. Taste. Adjust seasonings. Add cooked rice to cooked peas in the pot. Continue simmering until all the liquid has been absorbed.

FEBRUARY

MONTH OF THE HEART

This introduction is appropriate for older students.

"Your body is a fine machine. Your heart keeps your body going. Your heart pumps the blood through your body. Then the blood comes back through your veins (the little tubes your blood moves through). The blood comes back to your heart and it is pumped out and away through your body AGAIN. Every time your heart pumps, the vein stretches a little. This stretching is what makes your pulse. Your pulse tells you how fast your heart is beating. When you are well, your pulse is nice and steady. If you've been running, your pulse is fast. When you are sick your pulse may be slow.

"You can feel your pulse now. Put the inside of your middle fingers against the inside of the wrist of your other hand, below your thumb. Do you feel your pulse? How fast is *your* heart beating?"

Children are fascinated by the sound of a beating heart. Here is an easy way to make a stethoscope so that they may listen to heartbeats during this "month of the heart."

You will need an 18"-long rubber tube, two little funnels, and tape. Insert the long neck of the funnel into one end of the rubber tube. Tape it in place, if necessary. Do the same with the second funnel on the other end of the tube.

Let one child hold a funnel to his or her ear and put the other funnel against the left side of a friend's chest. Have the listener count out loud each time the heart beats (in 15 seconds' time). Then ask a second child to jump up and down twenty times. Replace the funnel onto the chest and ask the listening child to count out each time the heart beats. Why is the heart beating faster? (When you jump fast your body uses more energy and you make your muscles work. This means the blood must run faster and your heart is the pump that makes your blood run through your body whenever you jump high or use your muscles.)

NATIONAL MUSIC MONTH

If possible, bring some musical instruments to school. Present each one in a formal way so that children will have a serious attitude towards them. Obtain an outdated catalog of musical instruments from a local music store and let the kids find a picture to match each instrument you present. Let the children hear part of a tape or record of the music of each instrument you show them, if an actual musician should not be able to demonstrate each instrument.

You can cut out the catalog pictures of the instruments and glue them to faces of a deck of cards, and help them to play easy identification games such as Concentration* or cataloging them into the types of instruments: Strings, Woodwinds, Percussion, Brass.

*Concentration: Use cards with two identical pictures of each of five instruments. Lay these ten cards face down. Child turns up a card, names it, and turns up a second card. If the two match, child continues turning up a third and fourth card in an attempt to match these. If cards don't match, replace cards face down and second child continues game of Concentration.

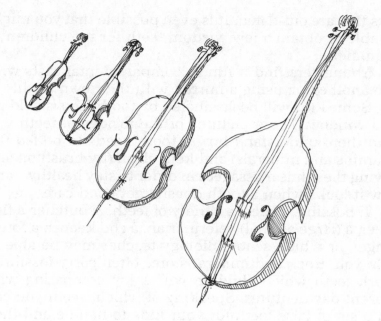

DENTAL HEALTH WEEK

This occurs during the first week of February.

Getting to Know Your Teeth

Let the children really LOOK at their teeth by studying them in a full length mirror hung sideways at their eye-level.

Ask them to see how many different tooth shapes they can find. The actual names of the different teeth are not important, but understanding what the different teeth do is interesting:

incisors (front teeth): cut or snip off food

cuspids (canine teeth): rip

bicuspids (2 teeth behind each cuspid): rip and tear

molars (back teeth behind bicuspids): grind and crush food

Older children may enjoy making each type of tooth into a person by making a simplified drawing and showing a balloon above telling what specific action it is best at performing. For example, a molar might say, "I am good at grinding. You use me when you chew popcorn at the movies!"

"Each of your teeth is covered by a very hard white coat that we call 'enamel.' Inside this hard cover is a soft part filled with nerves and blood vessels. The blood vessels carry food (vitamins and minerals) into your tooth to keep it strong and healthy. The nerves are like tiny telephone wires that send and receive messages back and forth from your brain. The nerves in your tooth can tell your brain: 'That soup is too hot' or 'Ouch, I just bit down on a nutshell!'"

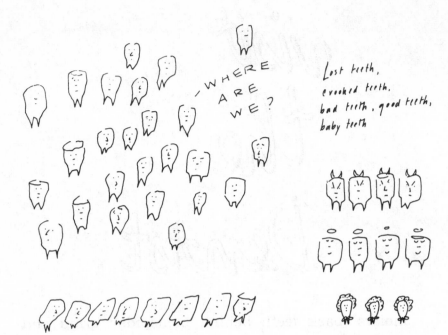

WHERE ARE WE?

Lost teeth, crooked teeth, bad teeth, good teeth, baby teeth

Good Dental Health Habits

What can you do to help keep your teeth healthy? (You can eat some raw vegetables every day; it's good exercise for your teeth to really *chew* some foods. You can drink milk or eat yogurt because they give your body calcium to help build up your teeth. And, of course, brushing and flossing your teeth keep them clean and free of the germs that destroy teeth if they get the chance.)

Your family dentist may provide an excellent source of teaching materials if you make your requests a few weeks before needing them filled. Ask your dentist if you might have several sets of dental casts (made from rubber impressions of different patients' mouths) or tooth X-

rays that are out-dated. It is even possible that you might be able to obtain a few wisdom teeth for the children to examine.

Youngsters find it fun to compare dental casts with one another, or, using a mirror, with their own teeth!

Some kids will be fascinated by tooth X-rays held up to a window. These pictures of the insides of teeth will help them understand how a tooth needs to be fed (by vitamins and minerals) and kept clean (by brushing and having the gums massaged) in order to stay healthy—and how it looks when a tooth doesn't get good care.

If possible, collect a variety of teeth. A butcher, a fish seller, a (large animal) veterinarian, a zoo keeper, a forest ranger, or a high school biology teacher may be able to help you. Rock and mineral stores often carry fossilized shark teeth which children will enjoy comparing with present day dentures. Speaking of which, see if you can get a set of false teeth for your kids to handle and then they might enjoy making some of their own.

A Macaroni Mouth

Provide each youngster with two 3″ × 3″ pink or red pieces of posterboard cut as shown here.

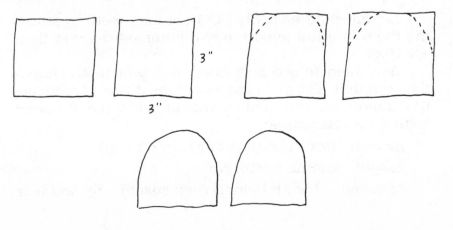

Give the students a bottle of white glue. Show them how to squeeze a line of glue all along the curved edge of the posterboard.

Next show them how to place "the teeth," small tube macaroni, open side down, all along the line of glue. The first macaroni "tooth" should be placed in front center followed by seven more teeth on that same side. The left hand side is then given eight teeth. When finished, each cardboard jaw should have sixteen macaroni teeth.

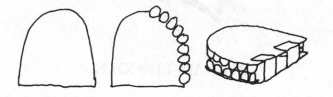

Ask each child to put the upper teeth on top of the bottom teeth, aligning them to get "a good bite." Use two pieces of pink or red cloth-backed tape to hinge the back of the macaroni mouth.

Have a good supply of old toothbrushes on hand so that several children at a time may practice brushing their pasta teeth in the correct way. Try showing them the wiggle approach: using a *soft* toothbrush, *wiggle* it up and down all along the gum line and between and behind your teeth! This wiggling motion stimulates the gums. "It helps bring blood to the gums and this keeps the gums and the teeth more healthy."

Getting to Know More About Your Gums

"Your gums are filled with tiny veins that bring blood to the roots of your teeth and feed them and keep them strong and really anchored in your jaws. The blood also takes away anything that your roots can't use, and this helps keep them healthy, too. If you gently rub your gums each night before you go to bed, this will help bring blood to your roots. And keep on brushing those teeth because brushing keeps your gums alive and well, too."

FREEDOM DAY

If you are working with older children, it may be interesting to question them about freedom on February 1, Freedom Day. Find out what they think "freedom" means. (Is a dog free? Are pets free?) Why is it good to feel free? When do you feel free? How are we not really free? (We must follow some laws; we aren't able to live without some grown-up helping us by giving us food, clothes, a house, and love.) Ask them for an example of someone, something that is truly free and then really examine their life and see in what ways it may not be free at all.

Freedom Day celebrates our country's right to certain freedoms. Briefly point out the fact that here in America we can say things and travel from state to state

and protect ourselves and family and read things in newspapers—all of these freedoms that many, many people in other countries are not allowed. If they seem interested in this subject, finally ask them to say what they think it takes to keep America free. (You don't have to comment at all on these ideas that they express. Such discussions offer them an opportunity to stretch their reasoning powers—and give you an opportunity to see these powers in action.)

GROUNDHOG DAY

"February 2 is called Groundhog Day. The groundhog is a medium-sized dark grey animal that lives in the ground. Another name for the groundhog is woodchuck.

"The groundhog was named by the Pilgrims—some of the first people from England who moved to our land. Remember their story back at Thanksgiving time? The Pilgrims called this animal 'groundhog' because it made them think of the little 'hedgehog' that lived back in England! They gave the groundhog here in America the job that their hedgehogs in England had. They are weather forecasters! They tell the farmers if spring is coming real soon or not for awhile … and today is the day that the groundhog should tell us how soon spring will be here. Guess how he does it.

"Early this morning the groundhog came out of his hole in the ground. He had been sleeping there all winter. The groundhog looked around. If it was cloudy out, he decided that spring would be here right away and so he left his hole for good. If it was bright and sunny this morning, the groundhog looked around and when he saw his shadow it scared him right back into his hole for another six weeks. This told the farmers that spring will be late this year … so don't try to plant your fields for six more weeks … !

"Look outside. What kind of day is it? Is it cloudy or sunny? Do you think the groundhog saw his shadow today?"

Go outside and see if you can find *your* shadows today.

ABRAHAM LINCOLN

"A hundred years ago our country had a very kind President. (A president is the person who is in charge of our country.) This President I'm talking about was tall and skinny. He was very kind and his kindness showed in his eyes: they were brown and twinkly. This man's name was Abraham Lincoln. His birthday is February 12, usually celebrated on the second Monday of the month.

"His name was 'Abe' for short. He was proud and happy to be our President and he worked hard to help our country. But Abe had lots of sadness in his life as you will hear.

"Abe grew up in the country. He lived in a cabin made of logs. He lived with his mother and father and sister. They were always poor. When Abe was still a boy, his mother died. He didn't get to go to school, like you, when he was little. And his family was too poor to have toys or story books for Abe and his sister.

"After awhile his Daddy remarried and his new wife helped Abe learn to read and write. Abe didn't have paper and pencils to write with like you and I do. Guess what Abe used when he was learning to write? He used pieces of charcoal from the fireplace and he wrote on flat boards or the wide part of a shovel!

"Abe had to work hard when he was young and he kept right on working when he got older. He worked so he could pay to go to school and learn to be a lawyer. A lawyer is a person who tries to help people who are in trouble.

"Finally Abe got to be a lawyer. He fell in love with a pretty, kind young woman and they were so happy together! But she died just before they were to get married. Abe was very very sad—for a long long time. But he did finally get married and have a family.

"Years went by. Abraham Lincoln got to be our President and he kept on helping people. We used to have black slaves in our country. Abe Lincoln didn't think it was right to keep people working when they didn't want to—and not even pay them money for their hard work! He helped all the black people to be free! That's why we remember Abraham Lincoln. He is called the President who freed the slaves!

"Today is his birthday, so let's make some honey cookies to celebrate this kind man's life!"

Honey Cookies*

(Make this dough in the morning. Chill it and cut out cookies and bake them in the afternoon.)

4 T butter) beat until soft
1 cup honey   )
½ tsp baking soda) add to butter; blend until creamy
1 egg   )
1 tsp vanilla) beat together
2 cups unbleached flour)
½ tsp baking powder   ) sift together
¼ tsp salt   )

Add a third of the flour mixture to the butter mixture. Then add a third of the egg mixture to the butter mixture. Repeat this procedure two more times. BEAT the batter after each new addition.

Chill dough until it is firm. Then roll it out onto a floured surface. Cut it into shapes using the hand-made cookie cutters described below.

Bake cookies on an oiled sheet in a 375° F. oven for about 9 minutes.

How to Make Your Own Cookie Cutters

Go to a building supply store and buy one (to three) yards** of four-inch flashing and a roll of smooth black electrician's tape. Use a yardstick and black felt-tip pen and divide the flashing lengthwise into one- and two-inch sections. Now use metal cutters and cut along pen lines. Three yard-long strips will result.

Use the electrician's tape to cover the cut edge of each flashing strip. This will protect the baker's fingers when cookies are being stamped out.

Each child will make a bold outline drawing on a piece of white paper. These may be hearts, crescent moons, a Lincoln top hat, a butterfly, a house, etc. Many youngsters may simply draw an abstract shape, which is fine, too.

---

*Abraham Lincoln enjoyed cookies like these. Honey was a big treat for kids in the early 1800's.

**One yard will make about 12 small cookie cutters.

Take a piece of string and go around the child's drawing, measuring the length of flashing that will be needed. Be sure to leave some extra to be overlapped later.

Cut off this length of flashing with which you will duplicate the child's line drawing. Stand the flashing atop the line drawing. Use needle-nose pliers to gently bend the metal until it exactly follows the line of the drawing. Overlap the two ends of the flashing. Wind the tape around both flashing ends, binding them together. Your handmade cookie cutter is now ready to use. Just wipe it clean with a dry cloth after each baking session.

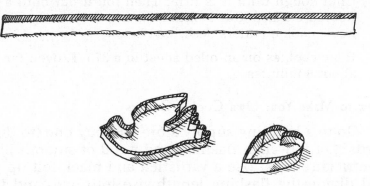

You may want to design and execute large cutters of your own! (You may want to invest in a small soldering iron if you plan large projects.) Maybe you would like to make a set of numbers or (some of) the letters of the alphabet. Children can then become familiar with these abstract shapes while involved in the wholesome activity of baking!

NATIONAL NEW IDEA WEEK

The second week in February is National New Idea Week. This is a perfect time to try out some new snack

ideas! How about letting the kids sample fried plantain or leaves from boiled artichokes or a selection of unusual raw vegetables from your market, e.g., jicama, or Chinese vegetables served with a dip of mayonnaise (or yogurt, sour cream, salt, and dill weed)? (See "February Recipes" for other new ideas.)

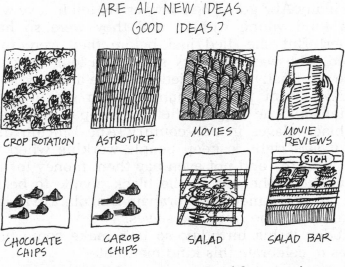

To help the children come up with some innovations of their own, provide them with a variety of empty thread spools, cardboard cylinders, broken clock parts, nuts, bolts, fine wire, and glue. Ask them to try and make (invent) their own robot people or mechanical people! Stay in the background and only help with technical problems; this is the best way to insure the flow of new ideas.

VALENTINE'S DAY

February 14 is Valentine's Day. There were several people named Valentinus in ancient history. Perhaps their lives have been consolidated into one story. No one is certain about the facts of *the* St. Valentine's life. But here is one version.

"Long ago in Rome there was a Christian* priest named Valentinus. In those days it was against the law to help or be kind to Christians. Valentinus was a good man and he gave help to anyone who needed it. Some of the

people he helped were Christians and so he was put in jail. The Romans said he must die. While he was in jail he met the jailer's little daughter. She was blind and she and Valentinus got to be friends. On the night before he had to die, Valentinus sent a goodbye note to the little girl. He signed it, 'From Your Valentine.' Today we send heart-shaped cards to our friends. Sometimes we say, 'From Your Valentine.' That means we like them a lot and hope they will like the valentine we're sending them."

Valentine Cards

Window Valentines: Provide a good selection of tiny red and pink hearts, tinfoil, little feathers, bits of lace, ribbon, sequins, and small glossy magazine pictures. Let each child select from these materials several things that he or she likes. Then he or she arranges these on a piece of waxed paper. A second piece of waxed paper is put on top and the two sheets are pressed together with a warm iron. **(CAUTION: Use the iron only under teacher supervision.)**

---

*Do you know what a Christian is? A person who believes that Christ was God's son and He came to live on earth to help people know God. The Romans had many different gods and they really hated Christians preaching that there was just *one* God.

Next give the children cards from which you have cut heart-shaped windows. Let the kids choose an area of their waxed paper collages and put it behind the heart-shaped hole and glue it in place.

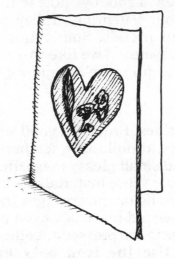

Valentine Variations: Kids love to create valentines from paper doilies and red and pink construction paper hearts (that you have pre-cut for very young children). Bring in colorful seed catalogs and scraps of appropriate gift wrap or a copy of the Metropolitan Museum of Art's Christmas Gift Catalog.* It has lovely colors and many angel pictures! Provide scissors and glue (and any help with cutting that is requested) and they will invent valentines that every parent will love!

Shiny Painted Valentines

Mix ®Elmer's Glue-All with diluted tempera paint. Let the kids use a variety of colors to achieve shiny valentine creations. You can sprinkle glitter along the

---

*255 Gracie Station, New York, NY 10028

edges or attach tiny seashells, butterflies, and ribbons to each card for really unique remembrances.

A Valentine Party

If your children are going to exchange valentines, make simple red paper folders for them to use to carry their cards and artwork home after the party. Be sure you send a card to each of the kids so that everybody will have something to put in the folder.

Make a group valentine and leave it for the mailman at your school. (You might enclose a couple of home-made cookies; this should help brighten the day *and* help the mail get through!)

Invite an elderly person(s) to tea. This might be a grandparent of one of the students or a helpful person in the neighborhood, such as the crosswalk guard. The children help prepare the snack and tea (or "champagne," recipe follows). Older children may serve guests and show them some examples of their recent artwork. A short puppet show or fairy tale play could be given. Finally, a big valentine made by the kids could be presented to each guest as he or she is getting ready to leave.

Valentine Party Treats

Layered Heart Cookies: Help the children roll out cookie dough and let them use heart cookie cutters of various sizes. Next they layer these, in graduated sizes, one atop the other, using a bit of egg white beneath each to insure that each layered cookie will retain its shape. These can be served with Kid's Champagne.

Kids' Champagne: Add 3-4 bottles of soda water to two large cans of frozen unsweetened apple juice. Keep this "champagne" in tightly capped (wine) bottles to insure retention of fizz. This is a good substitute for soft drinks.

Heart-Shaped Cake: If you should decide to bake a cake as a special valentine treat for your children, here's an easy way to achieve a heart-shaped cake. Bake one layer in a round cake pan and a second in a square cake pan. Cut the round (cooled) cake in half. Place one half up against one side of the square cake layer and the second half up against the adjacent side of the square cake. Voilà! A heart-shaped cake that now requires only frosting to keep it in shape.

GEORGE WASHINGTON

George Washington's birthday is February 22, usually celebrated on the third Monday of the month.

George Washington was the first President of our country. That means he was our first leader. We named the capitol of our country after him; it is called Washington D.C. We also have a state named Washington, and his picture is on some of our money. You can see George Washington on a quarter and on a one-dollar bill.

"George Washington was a quiet man. He was very honest. He worked very hard to help America become a free land. We call him The Father of Our Country."

George Washington's Fruit Cake

Here is a recipe for Washington's favorite fruitcake. His wife Martha made it for him. In fact they first received a cake like this from Martha's mother on their wedding day!

2 cups butter
2½ cups honey plus 1 tsp soda
5 eggs, separated and beaten
½ cup half and half
3 tsp baking powder
4 cups unbleached flour
1 cup currants, floured
¾ cup raisins, chopped and floured
a handful of orange peel, chopped fine and floured
cinnamon to taste
nutmeg to taste

Cream the butter and honey in a big wooden mixing bowl. Lightly stir in the separately beaten egg whites and yolks. Then blend in the milk. Sift the baking powder into the flour and stir this in. After these ingredients are mixed, stir in all the fruits and spices. Pour the batter into deep loaf pans or long shallow pans lined with well-buttered papers. George Washington's Fruitcake takes longer to bake than a plain cake. Bake at 275° F. to 300° F. for two hours or more; test cake with a toothpick for doneness. (Martha used a broom straw to test George's cakes!)

PURIM

Purim is a movable feast and may occur in February or March. It is a celebration marking the salvation of the Jews from the massacre planned for them by Haman, the advisor to the king of Persia. The story is told in the Biblical book of Esther.

"A young Jewish girl named Esther was raised by her cousin Mordecai in the land of Persia. The King of Persia fell in love with Esther and made her his queen. The King had an advisor named Haman. Whenever he had a problem, the King would ask Haman what to do. Well, Haman hated Esther's cousin Mordecai because Mordecai was Jewish and he would not bow down to him as all other people had done. Mordecai would only bow down to *God.* So Haman made a plan to have Mordecai and all the Jews in Persia killed.

"Esther learned of this plan. She invited the King and Haman to have dinner with her and when she told the King that Haman was going to have all her people killed, the King pitied her and she got him to protect her people from being killed by Haman."

During Purim the Jews celebrate Esther's bravery and sometimes make these Purim pastries.

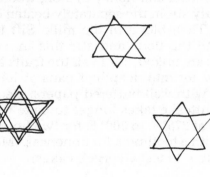

Hamantashen*

4 eggs	2 tsp vanilla
1 cup oil	3 tsp baking powder
1¼ cup sugar	½ tsp salt
5½ cup flour (approx.)	

Beat eggs, and beat in oil, sugar, vanilla, baking powder, salt. Add flour gradually, mix thoroughly.

Knead till smooth enough to roll on floured board. Roll out. Cut dough into 3″-4″ rounds. Place desired filling on each round. Pinch together sides of lower half of circles to form triangles.

Place Hamantashen on a lightly greased cookie sheet and bake at 350° F. for ½ hour, or until golden brown.

Fillings: The fillings are usually cooked prunes or mohn (poppyseeds). The prune filling may be made from (2 cups) cooked dried prunes with (½ cup) ground nuts and (1 T) grated orange rind added. Prepared pureed prune baby food or the mashed prune filling called *lekva* may also be used.

(Thank you again, Janie Stein Romero!)

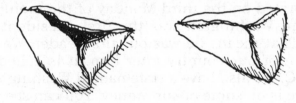

SNOW PROJECTS

Fun With Crystals

"Do you know how sand and salt and snow are all alike? No, this isn't a riddle. I just want you to learn something about crystals. That's how sand, salt, snow (and sugar) are alike—each one is a crystal.

"Crystals have flat faces and even shapes. Each snowflake is really made up of many tiny ice crystals. Every snowflake has six sides and no two snowflakes are ever

---

*Haman's hat pastries are made in a tri-cornered hat shape, a hat shape said to have been worn by Haman. This recipe is from "Guide for the Jewish Homemaker" by Shonie B. Levi and Sylvia R. Kaplan (National Women's League of the United Synagogue of America, 1964).

alike. Once in a while you might see really big snowflakes; they can be an inch across in size! That's because of the temperature outside. The colder it is, the smaller the snowflakes. So if you ever see big snowflakes falling, it's not very cold outside that day."

Here's a quick way to grow some ice crystals: pour some water on a sheet of glass and put it in your freezer. After a while, check on it and once it is frozen, take it out of the freezer. (If possible, have a magnifying glass handy to use to look at the glass up close!) You will see long flat needle-shaped crystals! They will melt real soon, so study these crystals *fast!*

If your kids are interested in growing some crystals at school, here are some things that will form crystals. All your children will need to do is let a solution of each evaporate and then they can examine, compare (and make little drawings of) the different crystals that are formed. Epsom salts, aspirin, alum, and bath salts can each be dissolved in water. Once the water evaporates, crystals will be left behind. If at all possible, use a magnifying glass to examine how each type of crystal really has a different shape.

Growing a Crystal Garden

Soak a synthetic sponge until it is very wet. Put it into a glass bowl. Stand some tiny twigs up in, or next to, the sponge. Mix together 4 T water, 4 T ammonia, and 4 T bluing. Pour this over the sponge. Let the children sprinkle one part of the sponge with *uniodized* salt. Finally, let some kids gently sprinkle on food coloring of different colors onto separate areas of the sponge.

Place the garden in a warm place, where it can't be disturbed. In a few days you will have a crystal garden growing at school! Add 2 T water and 2 T ammonia whenever the garden begins to get dry.

Growing Crystal Candy

Each child will need a drinking glass, a pencil or ice cream stick, a piece of clean string 6″ long, ½ cup of water, a paper clip, and granulated sugar. Tie the string to the middle of the pencil or stick. Tie the paper clip to the other end of the string. Put water in a pan and boil. Add sugar, one teaspoonful at a time, until no more will dissolve in the water.* Boil one minute. Pour this liquid into each glass. Place the pencil across the mouth of the glass, with a paper clip on the bottom of the glass. The glasses are then set in a warm spot where they won't be disturbed. Crystals will form in about a week. Break any crust that may form so that water will continue to evaporate.

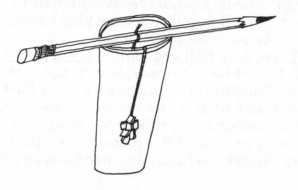

(You can gently tap one glass from time to time and see how this affects growth of crystals—how crystals in that glass are different from those in other glasses.)

---

*Generally speaking, one cup of water would be able to hold two cups of sugar.

FEBRUARY FIELD TRIPS

Take a nature walk and collect things that have specific geometric shapes. These may be natural forms or human-made. Try to get the kids "to see" a circle somewhere nearby, or a square, rectangle, diamond, triangle. Once you are back at school, separate the objects into different geometric groups and then into two groups: those that are made by people and those that are part of nature. Finally, look at each object and list the shapes seen within one object.

You may also, if it has snowed recently, look for tracks and try to decide *how* those tracks were made. (See "March Animal Tracks" for some specific examples.)

To celebrate National Music Month make arrangements to visit a local music store or music department at your high school. Encourage the children to ask questions and, if at all possible, let the kids have a chance to actually play an instrument or two.

Call your City Hall and inquire if you might bring the children to visit the city snowplow garage or large equipment lot. Children are impressed and excited by large machinery and what it can do. If you are fortunate and deal with someone empathetic to youngsters—and during a snow-free time of the month—the kids may get to climb up on some vehicles and maybe even get a ride!

ENRICHMENT OBJECTS

Nature Scope

This outstanding source of interesting wildlife teaching information is available monthly. Each issue has games, recipes, puzzles, and information, some of which is suited for very young children. Write, requesting that you be put on the mailing list:

Editor, Nature Scope
National Wildlife Federation
1412 Sixteenth Street, N.W.
Washington, D.C. 20036

(Order it now so that it will begin coming soon ... National Wildlife Week is in *March!*)

Presents for Children

The Metropolitan Museum of Art offers *Presents for Children,* a catalog that includes unusual books, such as, *Fairy Tales* by Terry Jones. These are 13 new fairy tales written by a member of the Monty Python team (C7832E), and musical instruments such as an xylophone of 15 accurately tuned movable metal pipes (upper C to lower C). These can be rearranged in different orders, and have a bell-like tone. Kit includes pipes, foam base, two wooden-tipped mallets and music for "Jingle Bells" (suitable for use with ages 3 and over) (M4927E). Write and ask that you be sent a current catalog:

Metropolitan Museum of Art
Museum Special Service Office
Box 700
Middle Village, NY 11379

FEBRUARY EATING EXPERIENCE

For an Ice Pudding Party, you will need a very good snowfall in order to present the children with this eating experience. If snow is unavailable, have a French Crêpe Party, using the recipe and directions at the end of this monthly chapter.

Explain to the children how people long ago did not have refrigerators, so they had to find other ways of keeping their food cold. Then, in the morning, prepare

Ice Pudding together, go out and bury it in the snow and, in the afternoon, share a dessert that was eaten 150 years ago in early America.

Ice Pudding

Boil 1½ pints milk with 1 tsp gelatin. Beat 5 eggs. Mix with milk. Oil a metal bowl and line with candied plums (or *well-drained* canned fruit*). Pour custard gradually into the bowl so that the fruit stays on the bottom of bowl. Cover the bowl with aluminum foil and top with an inverted metal pie pan.

Bury in the deep snow for one day. (The original recipe ends with: "Turn out at moment it is wanted.")

Or you can use small clear plastic cups and layer custard and (defrosted) cherries to make a cherry parfait on Washington's birthday!

FEBRUARY ENVIRONMENTS

A Dentist's Office

Clear (an area of) a room of all furniture. Then, following a trip to visit a local dentist, set a chair in the center of the room. Drape a white sheet over the chair. Place a floor lamp or gooseneck lamp next to the chair. Finally, stand a low table next to the chair and provide a metal dish (pie pan) of "tools," such as, chopsticks, plastic spoons, corks, and a white towel to put under the patient's chin.

A Beauty Salon or Barber's Shop

These can be made by simply providing appropriate plastic/wooden "tools," brushes, linens, and plastic wash basins.

---

*Pat fruit dry with a paper towel.

Emptied bottles (nail polish, shampoo, shaving lather, lotion) can be filled with lightly scented colored water.

Encourage the children to name their office or shop and (help them) make a sign to hang above the doorway.

FEBRUARY GAMES FOR INDOORS

Finger Shapes

Children sit in a circle. One child uses his or her fingers (and hands) to make the shape of a letter, a number, or an object such as a bowl, a hat, a ring, a basket, scissors, or a pipe. The other children try to guess it. (Keep this game moving right along and discontinue play as kids begin to lose their concentration.)

Object Charades

Begin the game by acting out a few common objects for the children, such as, a piece of bread in a toaster, tape, or an egg beater. Encourage the kids to speak in the way that the object might, saying whatever it might be thinking.

Whisper the name of an object to the first child and then you say, "I am thinking of something that…" and the child pantomimes the action of the object you whispered to him or her. The other kids try to guess the identity of the object from the first child's actions.

Once the object has been guessed, the game continues with another child acting out the actions of a *new* object. Some object suggestions are a pitcher pouring milk, a pencil writing a letter, a pair of scissors cutting paper, a doll being dressed or played with, a duck on a pond, a snowflake falling gently to earth, and a valentine.

Five Things in a Pillowcase

The first child reaches into a pillowcase and, without looking, removes one object. Then all the kids talk about the object, explaining how it is used and where it came from. This is repeated with each object in the pillowcase until it is emptied. Then the objects are put back into the pillowcase. Wait a few days, and then bring out the pillowcase once again. This time let the kids simply *feel* the objects in the sack and try "to remember" each one. (Objects might include a ruler, a carrot peeler, an empty pincushion, a nesting egg, a sponge, a bar of scented soap, an eraser, measuring spoons, and a feather.)

FEBRUARY PUPPET

The head and body of this hand puppet with movable arms can be made from a child's sock, a small box, or even an envelope. The child glues felt facial features onto the head area and adds yarn or raffia hair. (Details may be added to the body if you like.) Two small holes are cut below the face on either side of the body. The child slips

his or her hand into the puppet, forefinger in head and thumb and middle finger extended through the holes, thus becoming puppet's arms. With practice, the kids can learn to make their puppets scratch their heads, hold a tiny bouquet of flowers, drink from a thimble, clap, and turn pages of a book.

FEBRUARY RECIPES

E-Z Cheese Strips

Make a pie crust dough:

3 cups sifted flour
1½ tsp salt
1 cup shortening
6-9 T cold water

Gently mix the shortening into the flour and salt. Use table knives to cut in the shortening. Then add water until the dough holds together. Roll out the dough.

Cut strips 3 inches long and 2 inches wide. Cover each with grated cheese. Fold each strip in half lengthwise. Dust top of each strip with sifted cheese. Bake quickly at 425°F. until lightly brown and eat warm.

French Crêpes

Put 1 cup (cake) flour and ½ tsp salt into a bowl. Add 1 cup rich milk and 1 tsp vanilla. Add 2 eggs, dropping them in one at a time. Beat this until it is the consistency of a runny milkshake. Pour it into a pitcher. Place a (crêpe) skillet on medium heat. Add a bit of butter (you will do this before each crêpe is made).

Pour in a few tablespoons of batter. Tilt the pan to each side until the bottom is completely covered with a very THIN layer of batter. Turn crêpe with fork when edges are lacey. The first side will be golden and the second side will be pale. If this first crêpe is too thick, thin the batter with milk.

Spread jelly on the pale side of the crêpe and roll up into a tube shape.

Welsh Rarebit

Toast a slice of bread for each child. Let the kids use table knives to cut their toast into several pieces.

Boil water in a double boiler. Let the kids cut up cheese into little pieces. Drop the cheese into the top of a double boiler. Add milk to the cheese as it melts to give it a good consistency for dunking.

Remove the top of the double boiler from the stove and place it on the table. Let the kids spear their toast pieces with forks and dip into the warm cheese. (Ketchup can also be served in small side dishes for anyone who likes to then dip the cheese-covered toast into ketchup.)

MARCH

... In like a lion ...

NATIONAL DANDELION MONTH

Some kids may enjoy knowing that the word dandelion means "lion's teeth." It was named that because the edges of its leaves look like a lion's teeth!

People have eaten dandelion leaves for hundreds of years! Here is a recipe from 1894.

Dandelion Greens

A peck of dandelions will make one pint cooked.

Carefully look over each leaf.

Wash the leaves well in several water baths. Then lay the leaves in cold water for 20 minutes.

Bring a pot of water to boil. Add one tablespoon salt. Put in leaves. Allow to simmer 30-40 minutes, covered.

Drain leaves in a colander. Gently press out the water. Put them in a pan with one teaspoon butter and a bit of pepper. Cut leaves into pieces and mix well. Turn into a hot bowl with slices of hardboiled eggs. Serve with vinegar.

Dandelion Salad

Dandelions can also be eaten as a salad. Choose young leaves that are pinkish and still curled—before buds have appeared. Wash the leaves well. Chill them thoroughly before serving. These greens can be mixed with commercially grown lettuce so that the children have a chance to taste dandelions in a combination salad, rather than as a stark new flavor. Serve the salad with their favorite dressing.

Dandelion Tea

Let the kids pick older, large, *dark* green leaves. Put these into a paper bag. Place the bag in the sun for several days. When the leaves are dry, crumble them and put them in a jar—one teaspoon of leaves for each cup of tea to be brewed. Fill a jar with enough water for the number of cups of tea to be brewed. Place the jar, tightly sealed, in the hot sun for two hours. Add honey to taste.

Now find a spot to sit and sip your delicious Dandelion Sun Tea.

NATIONAL PEANUT MONTH

Peanuts—as well as coffee beans, grapes and figs—can be grown at school IF the seeds are green, unprocessed and have not been exposed to extreme temperatures. Sprout the peanuts in a jar that has moistened cotton or blotting paper right against the seeds. Moisten blotting paper (cotton) daily and keep the jar in sunlight. Once sprouted (and this may take as long as 2-3 months for some seeds) transfer the seedling to potting soil and plant ½″ down.

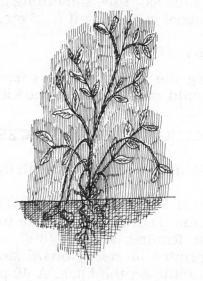

(It's good for children to have the opportunity to examine and compare a variety of young plants, their leaves, roots, and stems.)

Peanut Butter Bread

2 cups flour	1 cup peanut butter
2 eggs	1½ tsp baking powder
1⅓ cups honey	1 cup milk

Sift flour and baking powder together. Beat eggs, milk, and peanut butter together. Slowly add honey and mix well. Now add flour mixture. Stir.

Pour into a 9″ × 12″ pan. Bake 1 hour at 350° F. Cool. Cut into (25) pieces.

For a free recipe book on peanut and peanut butter baking, write to:

The Oklahoma Peanut Commission
P.O. Box D
Madill, OK 73446

ST. PATRICK

"Fifteen hundred years ago Patrick was born in Britain on March 17. He lived there with his mother and father until he was sixteen. Then one day when Patrick was playing on the beach, Irish pirates kidnapped him and took him away to Ireland. Do you know what 'kidnapped' means? He was stolen and forced to leave his home, even though he didn't want to.

"When he got to Ireland, Patrick became a shepherd. For six years he took the sheep into the hills to eat grass and brought them back at night to the barns. It was real sad and lonesome for Patrick. The only good thing that happened to him in those long years was that he thought more and more about God. He talked to God a lot and got very close to Him.

"Well, one night Patrick had a dream. In it he ran away from the pirates and a ship took him back home. The very next morning Patrick RAN AWAY! He walked for days and days until at last he came to the sea—and there was a ship! In the beginning the ship's captain didn't want to let him come on board, but at last he did. It took a long time, but finally Patrick got back to his mom and dad and he was HAPPY.

"For a while he stayed at home and then one night he had another dream. This time Irish people in his dream were calling him. They were saying, 'Come back, Patrick. Come back to Ireland. We *need* you!' Because of this dream Patrick went back to Ireland and he spent the rest of his life helping the Irish people. He taught them how to read and write and he helped them to know God. It is also said that he drove all the snakes out of Ireland."

Wearing o' the Green

Tell the kids that today everybody is supposed to wear some green because that color makes us think of Ireland and we remember St. Patrick today by wearing green. Then let each child cut out a little shamrock to pin to themselves to celebrate this saint's birthday.

Mix some green fingerpaint and/or bright green Play-Doh for a St. Patrick's art project.

A Green Walk

Take "a green walk": list all the green things you see as you walk and then once you're back at school, try and recall all the green things. Look at the list and give the kids hints to help them recall specific green things they have momentarily forgotten.

While on a "green walk" you might ask each child to find a different green object for the list or, once back at school, you could ask them to play a game of "I'm thinking of something green that we saw on our walk." The others try to guess its identity from the hints given after each wrong guess. For example, "Is it a car?" "No, it is part of nature." "Is it grass?" "No, it grows on a tree." "Is it a leaf?" "Yes!"

(This same format may be used for a guessing game inside school, such as, "I see something green." "Is it the rug?" "No, Michael is wearing it … ," etc.

St. Patrick's Snack

Try making the Green Potatoes (see "March Recipes"). They should *really* surprise the kids!

NATIONAL WILDLIFE WEEK

National Wildlife Week begins with the third Sunday of March.

The National Wildlife Federation (1412 16th Street, N.W., Washington, D.C. 20036) offers a full color animal photo kit that features sixteen (8½″ × 11″) excellent photographs printed on heavy board stock with a fact-filled animal profile on the back. A 40-page multi-level book of short stories featuring the animals pictured is included, too, as well as a handy 20-page Teacher's Guide to help you make the most of this useful kit.

Order #79904HA, "Wildlife in Your World Picture Series: Animals of North America." Inquire as to current price and shipping costs. This is a kit which you will find many occasions to use.

THE SPRING EQUINOX

March 21 or 22 is the Spring Equinox, or the first day of spring.

"Today there are just 12 hours of daylight and 12 hours of darkness, so it is a day of equal hours of darkness and light! Equinox means equal. Today is called the Spring Equinox!

"There is an old Greek story about today. Demeter and Zeus were two gods. They had a girl named Persephone. One day, Hades, the ruler of the underworld, kidnapped Persephone and took her down below the earth and married her.

"Well, when Persephone left the earth, the flowers died and the wheat all withered. Demeter, her mother, begged to have her girl returned. The Greek gods promised that Persephone could come back and live on earth for part of each year. When Persephone returns, all the plants begin to grow and life begins anew. The Greeks would say that this is the first day of *this* year that Persephone has come back to live on the earth with us again!"

What you will do to mark this day depends on where you live. If it is very warm and trees are already in bud, turn to the nature activities described in April. If it is still chilly and too early to plant a garden in your part of the country, continue reading the suggestions that follow.

Signs of Spring

Bundle up and go outdoors. Look around. "What new things do you see? Can you find any signs of spring? Do you see any new colors or new birds, perhaps? Can you find any signs of new life?"

Tracks

Look around in the snow or mud and try to find some tracks. These can be made by birds, animals, people, or objects. Encourage the children to identify and help you keep a list of all the tracks you see.

Animal Tracks

Cats (and foxes) walk in a straight line; they put their hind feet right in the tracks left by their front feet!

Dogs leave tracks on a pattern similar to a cat's but their hind feet don't hit exactly in the tracks left by their front feet. Compare tracks of a dog and cat and see what other distinctions the children can make. Can you see any nail-prints by each paw? How great is the distance between the front and back prints of each animal? (Bring a ruler and yardstick along on your walk.)

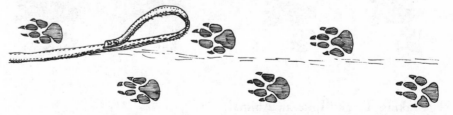

Rabbits and field mice put out one front foot and then the other front foot and finally they swing their back feet forward. Many times you can see a tiny line going up between the mouse's front and hind leg tracks. Can you guess what that is? ... Its tail!

Squirrels place their front feet down beside each other and then they swing their big back feet up in front of them. Lots of times you can see the track left by the squirrel's tail, too!

Once the tracks have been identified by the children, try to get them to study the tracks as a whole in order to answer such questions as:

Where was this animal (bird, person) going?
Why do you think it was going in that direction?
Was it going right across an open place or was it going along the edges?
WHY do you think it was walking in that way?
Was it walking or was it running?
Did it find anything? (food, another animal, a place to hide, or go to the toilet)
Which animal was bigger and how can you tell?

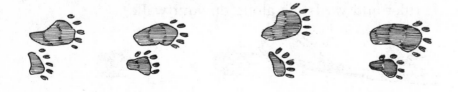

Making Tracks Like an Animal

Go outside after a light snowfall and encourage the kids to hop like a bird or a rabbit, or run like a dog, a fox, or a cat.

Making a Plaster Snow Cast

Put an inch of water in the bottom of a coffee can. Add two inches of snow. Pour in plaster of paris until it makes a peak one inch above the snow. Stir. The mixture should be like whipped cream (or you can add more plaster). Put a cardboard fence around a track and gently pour in the plaster so that it flows softly into the print. Let it harden for an hour or more.

EARLY SPRING'S INDOOR GARDENS

Fast-Sprouting Seeds

Fill the bottom of a jar with dried beans or whole wheat kernels. Cover the mouth of the jar with a square of cheesecloth and secure it to the jar with a rubber band. Now put the jar under a plastic bag to act as a humidifier. Every day pour some water through the cheesecloth onto the seeds and then pour off the water. Soon the seeds will begin to sprout. Get the kids to examine the progress of

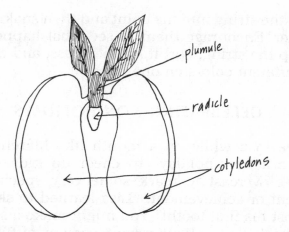

the seeds each day. Once the roots grow, the seeds can be transplanted so that a good root system may develop.

Everyday Vegetable and Fruit Seeds

Many common vegetable and fruit seeds will readily sprout for you and your children. However, your seeds will not sprout if they are sterile. For example, root vegetables, such as carrots, yams and white potatoes, may have been chemically treated to prevent their sprouting. Some fruits (raisins and dates) may have been dried at temperatures that sterilize the seeds. The seeds of chemically treated fruits may not sprout correctly either. So plant your random seeds and watch for sprouts. If none occur, plant a new seed from an organically raised fruit.

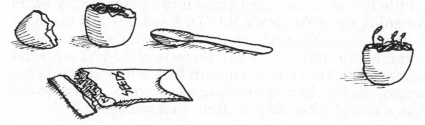

Orange, Grapefruit, and Lemon Seeds: Plant these ½" deep in potting soil (in a peat pot which can itself be planted in the ground once the seed has sprouted). Label each pot with the name of its seed and the date of planting. Put them in the sun and keep them moist until sprouted. This should happen in three weeks for grapefruit and five weeks for orange and lemon. When the sprout has formed, transplant it to a regular bed.

Banana Seeds: Banana seeds are not the little brown spots in the middle of a banana! Help your kids find the seeds of this fruit at the base of the banana where it meets the peel. A stubby inch-long "extension" of fruit that extends down into the base of the peel actually contains the banana seeds. Kids can scoop out this small tan protruberance and dissect it to discover the real banana seeds.

SPRINGTIME ART

Styrofoam Constructions

Collect a wide variety of styrofoam packing pieces—both big and tiny. Supply the children with toothpicks and finishing nails and hammers. Show them how these can be used to connect the styrofoam pieces together. Then just stand back and let them construct their own styrofoam sculpture.

An Easy-to-Make Loom

For each loom take an 8" × 10" styrofoam meat tray and make 1½" cuts at 1-inch intervals along the top and bottom of the tray; seven cuts at either end should result.

Next take a length of yarn and, leaving a foot for the final tying, thread yarn up through the first top slit and across the tray, going down through the corresponding

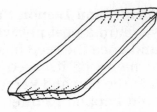

first slit at the bottom of the tray. Take yarn to the right and bring it up in the second slit at the bottom; proceed to take it back up across the tray going in the second top slit and under, coming up in the third top slit and going down across the tray to the third bottom slit, etc. Continue until all seven warp threads are in place.

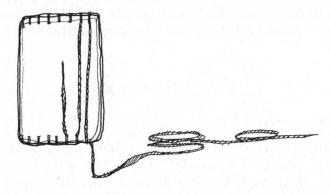

Tie off yarn ends firmly at the back of the tray. Now the loom is ready to use.

Besides weaving yarns of various colors and lengths on this loom, kids can use long feathers, leaves, pine needles, smooth twigs, long thin fabric scraps, or ribbons to achieve weavings that often seem like flat sculpture!

Painting with String

Provide saucers of tempera and string, yarn, and cord of different lengths. Let the children experiment with dipping the string into the paint and then snaking it over the paper. Encourage them to see what happens when you drop the string, curl it, roll it, press, and rub it. Try using different colors on one paper.

CELEBRATING NON-HOLIDAYS

Once in a while, in a month like March, perhaps celebrate a "non-holiday" to cheer up kids when the weather's overcast to mark some very special accomplishment or achievement. "Lisa learned to skip today! Jason lost his first tooth!" You might make a special tea party snack (how about crêpes? cream puffs? or Egg Drop Soup in March recipes) or you could celebrate by crowning the child Queen/King for the Day! (See "Easter" in the April section for the special hat suggestions.)

WINDY PROJECTS

What Makes the Wind Blow?

"It may sound funny, but the SUN can make the wind blow! Here's how it works. The sun comes out. It shines down and makes us warm. It also heats the air around us. Since warm air is lighter than cold air, the warm air goes up. Then cool air moves into the place the warm air left. This gentle moving in of the cool air makes a little breeze! If cold air *rushed* into a place left by warm air going up, we'd have a WIND. A wind is just air that's moving fast, and since the sun is shining and heating some air to make it go up, there is always some wind somewhere. March is the month that is famous for being windy. We say, 'March comes in like a lion ... and goes out like a lamb.' What do you think that means?"

Some Fun with 'Moving Air'

1. Look outside. What tells you that it's windy (that the air is moving) out there? (Smoke blowing from chimneys, trees tossing, clouds flying, birds' feathers ruffled, etc.)

2. Now go out the door. Lick your finger and hold it up. Which side of your finger feels cold? That tells you which direction the wind is coming from as it is blowing. Can you name the direction from which the wind is coming?

3. Now take a long thin piece of crepe paper and try running with it. Let it fly out behind you. Do you see how it is lifted off the ground by the wind going under it?

Pinwheels

Each child will need a square sheet of construction paper, a straight pin, a pencil with an eraser, a coin, a ruler, felt-tip markers, and scissors.

"To make sure the paper is square, fold the top right-hand corner across and over to meet the bottom left-hand corner. If any paper sticks out on an edge, carefully cut it off.

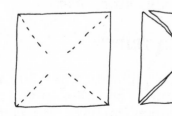 

"Now use your ruler to draw a line from one corner to the opposite corner. Draw a big X. Put your coin right in the middle of that X. Cover up where the two lines cross. Draw right around the coin to make a little O.

"This is the time to color any lines or designs you may want on the front and the back of your paper. You can color a different color inside each of the triangles that your pencil line X makes. Or maybe you want to draw stripes or zigzag lines on each triangle. Be sure to make it good and bright!

"Now cut the paper along each of the four lines. But DO NOT cut inside your little O at the middle of your paper. Bend every other corner into the center of the little circle. Now put a straight pin through the four corners and the middle of the circle. Then press the pin into the eraser on the end of the pencil.

"Try gently twirling your pinwheel with your finger. Does it twirl? Now blow into your pinwheel. You're ready to take it outside and watch the WIND make it twirl!"

A Wind Roarer

Let the older children help you construct these wind toys. Each child should measure and cut off 2 feet 6 inches of string. A knotted loop will be made at one end of the string for the finger to hold. The opposite end of the string will be tied to a thin 6-inch long piece of wood that has a small hole in one end. Experiment with different thicknesses of wood; let the children see if they can tell the difference in the sounds produced by a ¼-inch, a ½-inch and a ¾-inch piece of wood.

The finished wind roarer is taken outside—away from all other children—and the loop is held by one hand as the wood is twirled around child's head. As the string vibrates a howl is produced. (Will a shorter string make any difference in the sound produced? Try it.)

"Have you ever stood under some telephone wires on a windy day? They will make a howling sound just as your wind roarer does. Can you tell me why the wires make that sound? The wind is blowing through the wires and when they go back and forth real fast they begin to make howling sounds—just the way the strings on a guitar work to make sounds!"

MARCH GAMES

You Are a Leaf, a Bird, a Tree ...

When you've returned from a walk (or during the afternoon after a morning walk) have the children pretend they each are one of these: a leaf, a tree, a bird, or a blade of grass. Then ask them to show how they think they would move in each of the following situations:

1. It is softly raining and then the sun comes out from behind the clouds.
2. March winds are BLOWING!
3. A child walks up and touches you!
4. You are in the last snow of the year.
5. A child lets go of a kite and it flies right into you!
6. It is getting dark out and the moon is just coming up.

Nature Feely Boxes

Another activity that kids will enjoy following a nature walk is making and playing with Nature Feely Boxes.

Provide a pre-cut shoebox and lid for each child. Have each child select 2 or 3 items of nature from the things collected on their walk: seed pod, leaf, stone, twig, bone, pine cone, needles, feather, dried grass, bark, pebbles, moss, and nut. Offer a wide selection in each category. Each child will then place chosen objects in his or her box and replace the lid.

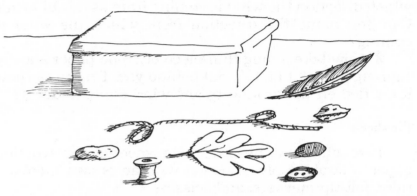

Friends will try out one another's boxes by inserting a hand, feeling contents, and then trying to guess the contents of the box. Encourage the use of descriptive words, such as, a smooth nut with a rough pointed end; a heavy, furry piece of moss; a long skinny feather.

MARCH FIELD TRIPS

Take a walk through your neighborhood and let each kid take a picture of something he or she likes. If you use an instant camera, let the kids (once you have returned to school) sort the photos and put them into sequence. Finally, make a book of the photos and ask them to tell you the story of your walk by "reading" the photos.

Contact a local metal sculptor or garden shop that sells wind chimes and bells, and arrange to have your children watch these wind bells being made. Other springtime field trip suggestions are: a visit to watch windmills, turbines or wind chargers; a trip to your local nursery now that it's spring; a visit with a chimney sweep; or a trip to watch a well being drilled.

ENRICHMENT OBJECTS

For a free seed catalog to help kids become better acquainted with a variety of plants and flowers, write to:

Burpee Seed Company
Warminster, PA 18891

Older children would be fascinated by the *Plant Discovery Kit* (#731 in the Edmund Scientific Catalog) available from:

Edmund Scientific Company
555 Edscorp Building
Barrington, NJ 08007

Two sources of free teaching materials concerned with peanuts are:

The Oklahoma Peanut Commission
P.O. Box D
Madill, OK 73446
(ask for a free copy of *The Lion Who Liked Peanut Butter*)

National Peanut Council
1000-16th St., N.W.
Suite 700
Washington, D.C. 20036
(ask for *The Great Goober Fun-Fact Folder*)

MARCH PUPPETS

Purchase several pairs of worker's gloves, the white cotton kind with the blue wrist bands, to make these quintet puppets. Use tiny felt scraps to make different people on the fingertips of one glove and various animals on another. You can glue the felt features to the tips, but ears should be stitched in place. Add yarn, ribbon, and feathers to give variety to these puppets.

MARCH EATING EXPERIENCE

Choose a chilly March day to prepare and then share this special recipe for hot cereal.

You will need cracked wheat (coarsely ground wheat) or rolled oats. If at all possible, provide the kids with examples of ripe wheat (oats) on the stalk and (let them rub off) the whole kernels so that they can see how grains look before they are cracked, ground, or rolled. Your children may, in fact, enjoy using a wooden mortar and pestle (or rolling pin) to produce their own cracked wheat or rolled oats!

¾ cup powdered milk ("How do you think milk can be changed into a powder? All the water, wetness, in it is taken away. Why would we want to change wet milk into a powder? When milk is a powder it won't spoil. You can keep it longer.")

3 cups water
½ cup chopped apples, raisins or nuts*
1 tsp salt
honey or brown sugar
whole milk

Bring the 3 cups of water to a boil in the top of a double boiler. Turn heat to medium. Stir 1½ cups of grain into the boiling water. Stir carefully, slowly, and constantly. See that all the grain is coated with water. Now stir in the powdered milk and salt. Continue cooking until your cereal becomes thickened. ("Why does the cereal change from runny to thick? The kernels of grain take in water and swell up to make the cereal thick.")

Add fruit and/or nuts to all or part of the cereal, according to the children's tastes.

Scoop out small portions into waterproof paper cups or bowls. Add a little brown sugar or honey to each portion as desired. Pour some milk onto each serving of this homemade hot cereal. (NOTE: Ceres was the Roman goddess of agriculture. Our word "cereal" means "from Ceres" because it is made of grain or the grasses that give us grain.)

MARCH ENVIRONMENT

To make a see-through tent, purchase several yards of heavy duty plastic. Make the tent indoors by draping it over a low slung rope suspended between two walls. Hold the sides of the tent to the floor by placing bricks along the edges of the plastic. An indoor variation is made by covering a small table with the plastic, letting the edges hang down to form the tent walls. Or place two chairs back to back several feet apart and lay plastic over them, weighing the plastic in place by putting heavy books on the plastic atop the chair seats.

An outdoor see-through tent is lots of fun—especially during a gentle rain! Drape the plastic over your clothesline and weigh down the edges with stones. Kids love playing in this see-through playhouse.

MARCH RECIPES

Egg Drop Soup (Tan Hua Tang)

2 cans chicken broth
1 large ginger root, peeled and slivered
4 eggs
4 T chopped green onion
2 T chopped fresh parsley

Bring the chicken broth to a boil. Drop in the ginger root. Help the kids beat the eggs until frothy. Help the children use spoons to drop the egg—a little at a time—into the hot broth.

("What shapes do you see coming up to the top of the soup? What does that egg shape look like?")

---

*Take a vote now to be sure that it's all right with everyone to add fruit and/or nuts.

Kids do not always readily appreciate a new recipe or an unfamiliar texture, so it's wise to start off by serving small portions.

Carefully ladle small amounts of soup into little bowls or waterproof paper containers.

Let the children garnish their soups with onions or parsley as they like.

Green Potatoes

This recipe is good for St. Patrick's Day or any day there's a nip in the air.

6 medium-sized potatoes
3 stalks broccoli
¼ cup milk
2 T butter
1 tsp salt
¾ cup grated cheese (Monterey Jack, cheddar, mozzarella, or a combo)

Peel the potatoes and boil or steam until done. Peel off the tough outer skin from the lower broccoli stems. Steam the broccoli until just tender. Chop fine and put into a bowl.

Mash the potatoes until they are free of lumps. Then add them to the broccoli. Add ½ cup of cheese, butter, salt, and milk. Mash all these ingredients until

potatoes are pale green with flecks of dark green. If mixture is no longer warm, return to the stove briefly. Serve green potatoes warm with a sprinkling of the remaining cheese. (You may prepare this recipe by omitting cheese and slightly increasing broccoli and butter.)

Irish Soda Bread

2 cups whole wheat flour
1 cup unbleached flour
1½ tsp salt
¾ tsp soda
½ cup corn oil
¼ cup brown sugar
¼ cup molasses
1 egg
1½ cups sour milk or buttermilk
1½ cups currants
1½ cups raisins

Preheat the oven to 325° F.

Sift or mix together all dry ingredients. Then cream oil, sugar, and molasses together. Beat in the egg.

Add alternately: dry ingredients with buttermilk. Stir in the raisins and currants.

Pour the batter into a greased 8″ × 4″ × 2½″ loaf pan, or butter five 1-lb. coffee cans and fill each ¾ full. Bake about 75 minutes.

APRIL

APRIL FOOL'S DAY

Young children may not understand how/why jokes played on April 1 are thought to be funny. You might mention to your kids that in France people who get fooled today are called April FISH because they are easily caught. You might celebrate today with these gentle jokes.

YOUR SHOE IS UNTIED

YEAH, SURE

Silly Sentences

Say one of these sentences and then wait for giggles and an explanation of what is silly about what you've just said: "I like Easter because that's when Santa Claus brings me Easter eggs!" Then try the following:

I cut my finger and my big toe bled.

Farmer Brown's horse gives wonderful milk.

This morning I saw lots of dogs singing in the trees.

Tonight you'd better be careful or you'll get a moon-burn!

My favorite dessert is chicken soup!

April Fool's Day Art

Have the children wash their hands. Lay a sheet of glossy (butcher's) white paper in front of each child. Use a big spoon to put dabs of vanilla pudding dyed with berry juice to become blue or pink or purple onto each piece of paper. Watch to see how/when the children discover the April Fool part of this art project!

HANS CHRISTIAN ANDERSEN

"Hans Christian Andersen was born on April 2 in 1805 in Denmark. His father was a poor shoemaker and died when Hans was a little boy. Hans didn't get to go to school when he was little, but he did read lots of books. He loved to read plays and stories, and a few years after his daddy died, Hans left home to go to the big city of Copenhagen. He thought that he would like to sing in plays in the city, but he could not get a job because—for one thing—he was only fourteen! It was a very hard time for Hans and he almost starved to death. At last two

musicians and a poet found him and took him home and took care of him.

"After awhile Hans wrote a small book about ghosts. The King of Denmark read it and liked it so much that he gave Hans money to use to go to school!

"Hans wrote more stories. The King enjoyed them so much that he gave Hans money as long as Hans lived. Do you know some of the stories that Hans Christian Andersen wrote? He wrote *The Ugly Duckling*, *The Tinderbox*, *Little Claus and Big Claus*, *The Tin Soldier* and *The Little Match Girl*."

Check out a collection of Andersen fairy tales and share a few appropriate ones with your children.

Have the children work together painting on a long piece of (butcher) paper (parts of) the story of *The Ugly Duckling*.

INTERNATIONAL CHILDREN'S BOOK DAY

April 2 is also International Children's Book Day. Since Hans Christian Andersen was born on this day, let your students explore his many stories.

PASSOVER

Passover is a movable feast and occurs in the spring. It is the Jewish holiday that celebrates the liberation of the Jews and their exodus from Egypt. It is a celebration of freedom.*

A traditional dinner, the seder, is held on the first night(s) of Passover. Before the meal, the Haggadah is read, telling the story of the Jews' flight from Egypt.

"Long, long ago when the Egyptians were building their pyramids, they used Jewish slaves to cut the huge stones and move them and pile them up with mortar in between to hold the stones together. The Jews did not *want* to be slaves. Their life was very hard. Their leader was named Moses and he asked the Egyptians to let the Jews go home. But the Egyptian pharoah (their leader) said, 'No! You must stay and work for US! You are our slaves!'

"Well, Moses talked to God, and then he went back to the pharoah. 'If you don't let the Jews go, God will make bad things happen to you!' Then, because the Egyptians

---

*If you are not Jewish, consider inviting a Jewish parent(s) to your classroom to share stories or special foods.

still wouldn't free the Jews, God made many bad things happen to the Egyptians. The sun didn't shine, the water was all bloody, and then slimy lizards and snakes covered everything!

"Finally God told the Jews, 'Tonight each of you must mark an X on your door so your family will be passed over when some really bad things happen.' That night was terrible for the Egyptians. In the morning the pharoah told the Jews that they were not slaves anymore and they could leave and go home again. The Jews were so happy and left Egypt as quickly as they could! They were free at last!"

During the seder, ceremonial foods are included as part of the dinner:

Bitter Herbs (Horseradish)—symbolize the bitterness of slavery.

Charoses—made from apples, raisins, and sweet wine. It is meant to resemble the mortar used by the Jews laying the bricks for the pyramids. It also symbolizes the sweetness of freedom.

Three Matzos (unleavened crackers)—symbolize the haste of the departure of the Jewish people from Egypt. There was no time to leaven the bread. The *three* matzos also represent the three ancient Jewish religious groupings.

Roasted Shankbone—symbol of the pascal lamb offered in sacrifice at the Temple.

Roasted Egg—the second offering brought to the Temple on Passover. The egg also symbolizes the cycle of life and death, freedom and bondage.

Karpas (a green vegetable such as parsley)—a reminder that Passover comes in the spring and is a time of new life.

You might like to prepare Charoses with the children. Here is a simple recipe.

Charoses (Har-osez)

6 medium-sized apples, grated
½ cup raisins soaked overnight in orange juice
½ tsp cinnamon
¼ cup sweet wine (or frozen orange juice concentrate)
½ cup walnuts, chopped finely

Mix all the ingredients well. Refrigerate the Charoses until served.

GOOD FRIDAY

Your children may ask why this day is so named. "This day was really named God's Friday. It is a very serious time for Christians because it was on the Friday before Easter that Jesus was put on the cross where he died.

"When it is Easter, it will be a happy day for Christians because that is the day that they remember how Jesus came alive and went up to Heaven."

In England every Good Friday is greeted with the making and savoring of hot cross buns. You may enjoy making and sharing them with the children.

Hot Cross Buns

2 cups flour	1 cup milk (or less)
1 T dry yeast	¼ cup brown sugar
½ cup currants	2 eggs, beaten
1 tsp salt	¼ tsp each: cloves, cinnamon
softened butter	allspice, nutmeg

Warm the milk and soften the yeast in a bit of it. Warm the flour in a bowl. Then add sugar, salt, and spices.

Make a well in the flour and stir in yeast, butter, eggs, and as much milk as it takes to give dough a firm consistency. (You can knead raisins or bits of citron into the dough.) Cover bowl and let dough rise until double in bulk. Punch down. Turn onto a floured board. Knead a bit. Form into 24 round buns and place 2″ apart on an oiled cookie sheet. Allow to rise until doubled. Just before baking cut a cross in the top of bun.

Bake at 400° F. till brown. Cool a bit. Trace the cross with a thin icing of ½ cup sifted powdered sugar, ½ T warm milk, and ½ tsp lemon juice.

NATIONAL LIBRARY WEEK

National Library Week begins with the second or third Sunday of the month. Write to the National Book Committee at:

1 Park Avenue
New York, NY 10016

Inquire as to this year's dates.

Certainly contact your Public Library and ask about any planned special programs and events which your children might enjoy.

EASTER

The three main happenings that Christians celebrate each year are: the birth of Christ, the crucifixion, and His resurrection. Easter, a movable feast, is the holiday that marks the last two events.

The secular parts of Easter include the Easter bunny, eggs, baskets, egg hunts, and bonnets. These include symbols that young children especially enjoy.

A Paper Plate Bunny

Place two thin paper plates atop one another with the insides of the plates facing each other. Use a hole puncher to punch holes through the two plates an inch inside the plate edge and all around the plates, leaving a 6-inch area without holes.

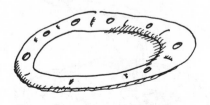

Now give each child a large #4 blunt-ended needle* threaded with a long piece of yarn, the ends of which you have knotted together. (You may thread a button onto the yarn before the child begins to sew to insure that stitches will not pull out of the plate.) Now each child will sew the two plates together, leaving a hole at the bottom of the plates. Two long pink (lined) ears are cut from paper and stapled to either side of the head. Leave a hole at the bottom of the plates. Next have the kids paint or cut and paste rabbit features onto the surface of each plate.

Finally, the child inserts his or her hand through the hole at the bottom head and animates the paper plate bunny.

These Easter rabbits are also simply fun to use as decorations during spring.

An Easter Bunny Cake

Bake a chocolate or carob cake in a round cake pan. Allow the cake to cool completely. Remove the cake from the pan and cut it in half producing two half circles. Put a cream cheese and orange juice frosting between the

layers and then, flat sides down, stand them side by side on a large plate. Two inches up from the plate, cut a 2-inch wedge out of the cake.

This is joined with icing to the rear of the cake to become the tail. Frost the entire cake with a cream cheese or frothy white icing and sprinkle liberally (except for the tail) with unsweetened coconut. Add carob-covered raisin eyes and a pink jellybean nose and short black licorice-whip whiskers. Two construction paper ears will complete your Bunny Cake. (See "April Puppets" for two other Easter bunny ideas.)

Easter Bunny Painted Cookies

Use a large rabbit cookie cutter to cut out cookie shapes from a favorite roll-out cookie recipe.

Put drops of 4-6 different food colorings into 4-6 custard cups or clean baby food jars. Pull the outer membrane sac from two egg yolks and add some of the yolks to each cup or jar. Mix the colors well. Mix ½ tsp water with the egg yolks. Kids use small (new or very clean) paintbrushes and paint designs on their bunny cookies before they are baked according to the recipe used.

---

*Prepare these needles, one for each child, in the morning before school starts so that you'll be all set to begin this project together.

Coloring Easter Eggs

To hard boil eggs so that they are easier to peel and will have less green around the yolk, cover the eggs with heavily salted cold water. Be sure that the eggs are not crowded in the pan. Cover the pan and bring water to the boiling point and then turn off the heat, leaving the covered pan on the stove for 15 minutes. Then immediately submerge the eggs in cold water.

Add a tablespoon of vinegar to each cup of (food coloring) egg dye to give vivid tones and to set the color.

A Very E-Z Method for Dying Easter Eggs*

Collect styrofoam egg cartons and separate into sections of four egg cups to a section. Squirt a food coloring of different shades into each of the egg cups. Provide children with cotton swabs and hard-boiled eggs and let them apply dye directly to the egg. Allow coloring to dry completely before handling.

Banded Eggs. Wind rubber bands or thin strips of masking tape around the hard-boiled egg. Dip the egg into the dye. Allow the egg to dry. Remove the rubber bands or tape. (The egg may be given a coat of dye prior to wrapping bands/tape around it and then dipped in a new color to achieve a two-tone banded egg!)

Frosted Egg. Let kids draw with light colored crayons on a hard-boiled egg. Then the egg is dipped into a dye bath.

Marbleized Eggs. Mix powdered paint with linseed oil. Pour warm water into a large shallow pan. Dip a small paintbrush into the oil and paint mixture and spritz it onto the surface of water. Children roll their eggs in the water to achieve a marbleized effect. Use kitchen tongs to remove the eggs to an egg carton to dry thoroughly before handling.

Bejeweled Eggs. Provide kids with a wide variety of tiny cloth and ribbon pieces, lace snippets, and a variety of colored sequins. Let them glue these flat (and overlapping) to the surface of hard-boiled eggs.

Leaf-patterned Eggs. For each egg to be dyed, cut a 5-inch square of nylon stocking. Place a small flat leaf (geranium, fern) or flat flower or petals** in the center of the nylon square. Place an uncooked egg right on top of the leaf. Gently and firmly pull the nylon tightly up and around the egg. Tie the nylon tight with a piece of string.

Carefully lower the eggs, one at a time, into the dye pot. Simmer gently in an uncovered pot for 20 minutes. Use a slotted spoon to lift out the eggs and submerge in cool water until just cool enough to handle. Untie the nylon covering and remove the leaf. Let the egg dry.

When dry, rub the egg with a few drops of salad oil until the surface of the egg has a soft glow.

Natural Dyes for Eggs.*** Pioneer children used vegetation to produce Easter egg dyes. You can, too, and

---

*Thank you, Mrs. Dru Barclift!

**Any thin flat opaque objects can be substituted for leaf: try gummed stickers, little plastic cut outs, snowflake-shaped sequins, etc.

***Experiment with other colors by adding yellow onion skins (or grass) to water = yellow, chestnuts = blue, blackberries, concord grapes = purple, rhubarb leaves = green, and sassafras root, bark (available at health food stores) = orange.

your children should be fascinated by the procedure: Add a tablespoon of vinegar to the juice from a can of beets. Bring to a boil. Carefully add eggs. Simmer ten minutes. When cool, eggs are polished to a high sheen with a bit of salad oil.

Silly Egg Heads

Save egg shell halves and place the round ends in an egg carton. Let each kid draw a face on a shell with a felt-tipped pen and then fill the egg head with a mixture of soil and vermiculite. It's easier to fill the egg shells if kids spoon the mixture into them. Grass seeds are sprinkled on top of soil and then watered with a spray bottle filled with water. The soil must be kept damp, so encourage the kids to keep a daily check on the carton.

In a few days each egg head will begin to grow a fine green crewcut!

Finger Jell-O Eggs

Collect egg shells (or blow out contents of enough eggs to provide one for each of your children) and rinse them thoroughly. Let shells stand overnight. Fill with Finger Jell-O (see "April Recipes"). Allow Jell-O to harden and then let children crack these eggs, and enjoy the contents!

Easter Baskets

(See "May Baskets" for other suggestions.)

A Quickie. Punch a small hole near the top edge on either side of a cottage cheese container or margarine tub. Insert a large fuzzy pipe cleaner through one hole and bend over the container to form a handle. Insert the other end of the pipe cleaner through the second hole and twist the ends to secure the handle in place. The child will use the basket to collect tiny Easter goodies which you have hidden around the yard or room.

Living Easter Baskets. You will have to start these baskets one week before Easter as it takes that long for them to grow.

Line a commercial berry basket with a 5″ × 5″ piece of plastic wrap. Pour ½ cup of vermiculite into the lined basket. Sprinkle two teaspoons of wheat berries on top of the vermiculite. Pour ½ cup of water on (until water shows under) berries. (You will water the basket just this once.)

Now place the basket near a window. Completely cover the top of the basket with plastic wrap. After two days remove the plastic wrap.

Hide a few Easter goodies in the wheat berry grass on the day that the basket will be used. If you want to add a handle, staple a 2″ × 15″ strip of poster weight cardboard to the side of the basket, loop it down, and staple to the opposite side.

Easter Bonnets, Hats, and Crowns

A Basic Hat-making Technique*. Mix white flour and water to form a paste. Use this to glue two large sheets (20″ or more) of butcher paper together. While the pasted paper is still wet, shape it to the child's head to form the crown of the hat. Tie yarn or a ribbon around the paper to make it hold this crown shape. Now trim and shape the brim of the hat to any style you choose: firefighter, cowboy, baseball player, the bowler worn by the Irish, or a floppy brimmed hat worn in the Gay Nineties! Allow paper to dry thoroughly and then paint/decorate appropriately.

---

*Thanks to Dixie Arter Hyde!

Party Hat. For each hat, take a long piece of paper and fold up a 2-inch flap along one side to form a head band and give the hat added strength. Make 15 slits along the other side of the paper. Now fit the headband around the child's head and overlap the ends of the paper. Staple the ends in place. Gather all the 15 strips together at the top of the hat. Insert crepe paper streamers of a contrasting color and bind them all in place with a colorful piece of yarn!

Mercury's Winged Hat. Take a 4-inch wide strip of purple paper and fit it around the child's head. Staple the overlapping ends of paper. Reinforce with two overlapping lengths of paper stapled to the crown of the hat. Finally, have the child draw two large wings. Cut these out and glue one to either side of Mercury's hat.

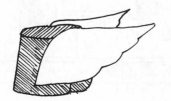

Crowns. Accordion-pleat a length (circumference of child's head) of gold-foil wrapping paper and cut out this shape. Bend the tallest flanges over and staple together to form the top of the crown. Decorate with bejeweled buttons or squares and diamonds of colored foil.

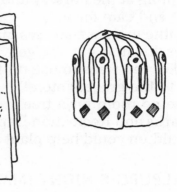

Variations. Accordion-pleat a length of paper and cut out various shapes. Staple the ends together and decorate.

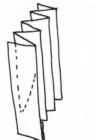

EARTH DAY AND EARTH WEEK

April 22 is Earth Day and the week encompassed by it, Earth Week, celebrates the equinoxes and stands for balance and harmony on earth.

ARBOR DAY

Arbor Day is sometimes celebrated on April 22, but the date varies from state to state.

What a perfect day to plant a tree together. You may buy a small sapling at the nursery and get advice on how best to plant it and care for it.

"Trees breathe in a gas that cars make. This gas turns to smog. Trees breathe out oxygen and THAT makes clean air. It takes ten trees to use up the smog made by one car going to the grocery store!"

If you have no room for a tree at school, you might call the City Parks and Recreation Department and ask if you and the children could help plant a tree for your city.

WALPURGIS NIGHT (MAY EVE)

Taking place on April 30, this is the first of the three festivals traditionally celebrated by the fairies. (Midsummer Eve and Halloween are the other two.) Tonight the fairies are said to sing, dance, and make merry, welcoming back warm days and new life.

Dancing to a Music Box

Ask the children to pretend that they are the fairies, dancing to welcome back spring days. Tell them that as long as the music box plays, they may move, but whenever the music stops, they must also. Wind the box so that it plays for different amounts of time. Provide the children with silken scarves to float in the air as they dance. (Use 2-3 music boxes with different songs.)

RAINY DAY NATURE STUDIES

Why Does It Rain?

"There is a gas in the air that we cannot see. This gas is called water vapor. When warm wet air rises up from the ground, it makes the water vapor turn into tiny little drops of water. These tiny drops all get together and make a cloud.

"When the water vapor in the cloud makes bigger and bigger drops of water, the cloud just gets heavier and heavier. It begins to look black. (You've seen a big black cloud in the sky sometime, haven't you?)

"Well, the drops in the cloud get heavier and heavier until they are too heavy to stay up in the sky and then they fall down out of the cloud and we say it's raining."

Making Rain

"We can make some rain right here in school. First we boil a pan of water. **(CAUTION: Take every precaution to see that no one gets hurt by the steam or water involved in this activity!)** Then I'll put on a hot mitt to protect my hand. I'm going to hold a glass pie plate over the pan, but not touching it. What do you see beginning to happen? (Steam is beginning to cover the plate.) Now what do you see is happening? (Little drops of water are sliding off the plate and falling back into the pan.)

"Well, that's just how we get rain! Water gets warm and it goes up into the sky. When lots of water drops get together, you have a cloud. When the clouds gets too heavy, the water drops fall back down to earth. It's that simple."

Looking at Leaves (Insects) Up Close

Borrow an opaque projector from the audio-visual department of your school, public library, community college, or local school district. (Have the children help you collect a variety of leaves and dead insects.*) Darken the room. Place a leaf on the flat surface of the projector. Quickly describe its shape and then place a second leaf on the projector. ("How are the two leaves different? Yes, that's right, one is long, smooth and thin, and one is flat with sides that go in and out. Now how are these two leaves alike? They both have a stem; they're both green, they both have a line down their middle," etc.) Be sure to use words that are specific: stem, veins, margin (outer edge of leaf), and tip.

Let (older) children draw several different shapes of leaves.

If dead insects are available, lay each on the flat surface of the projector. Notice the legs, wings, and antennae of each. Compare one insect with another. If they want, let older children draw several of the insects.

"How are insects and leaves alike?" (You should get some interesting answers to this one.) "How are they very different?" (Accept any feasible answers or connections they make no matter how surreal ...) "How do leaves and insects use each other?"

Making Leaf Imprints

Go outside with the kids right after a rain. Let each one find a leaf and gently press it, vein side down, into the damp firm mud. Leave it there and go away for awhile, until the mud has had time to dry out a little. When you return, each child will carefully lift up the leaf and see what has happened to the mud. (If possible, have some actual fossil samples available so that the kids can compare their leaf imprints with the ancient prints left by leaves and creatures in muds of a million years ago.)

Go back inside and let the children make leaf (and shell) imprints using plasticene clay.

A Homemade Barometer

"A barometer measures air pressure. When we're having good weather, the air pressure is usually high. When the air pressure falls, it's a sign that the weather is changing. Lots of times when the air pressure falls it means there's going to be some bad weather soon."

---

*Look inside an outdoor light fixture or between the screens and windows of your school.

You and your children can make a barometer that will show air pressure. Glue a long thin strip of paper to the outside of a glass (milk or cream) bottle.

Fill the bottle three quarters full of water. Tightly cover the bottle's mouth as you invert the bottle into a water-filled pan. Stand the bottle upside down. Don't uncover the bottle's mouth until the bottle is completely submerged beneath the water.

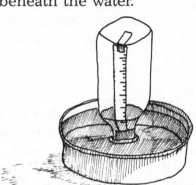

Since changes in temperature will make air (in the bottle) expand or contract, you must keep the bottle in a place where the temperature is quite stable, such as in a closet. As the water climbs or falls in the bottle, mark its level on the paper. In this way, the strip becomes a barometric gauge.

Help the children to observe the weather with each change of their barometer and to make generalizations accordingly.

FUN WITH WIND PROJECTS

Flying Streamers

Cut long narrow strips of cloth from an old sheet. Staple long crepe paper streamers of different colors all along one edge of each cloth strip.

Have a child hold one end of the cloth strip in each hand and run wildly across the yard with the flying streamer soaring out behind. This makes a wonderful windy weather toy!

Parachutes

Cut lightweight cloth or plastic into squares. Tie each corner of the square with a piece of lightweight string (the length of one side of your square). Gather the four loose ends of the strings together and tie them to a small object that the child chooses, such as a button or paper clip or a tiny cut-out of a person the child has drawn on lightweight cardboard.

Now each kid can throw the parachute up in the air—and the wind will do the rest!*

Wind Chimes

Little children enjoy constructing and then listening to these handmade wind chimes. Tie long strings of varying lengths to a variety of six-penny and twelve-penny nails. Hang the strings close together from a 10-to-12-inch long dowel. Tie the dowel in turn to a tree limb and enjoy your wind chimes with every passing breeze. (Try making other wind chimes by hanging canning jar lids and rims or the lids from a variety of tin cans from a dowel.)

APRIL FIELD TRIPS AND VISITORS

Phone your local Agricultural Extension Service. Arrange to have a specialist come by and provide you

---

*Cut out a tiny square from the exact center of the square. This will help the parachute fall straight. Let the kids try it both ways and compare the results.

with information on small gardens, the soil next to your school, and composting. With the children's help, plant a mini-garden. Include the old favorites: radishes, string beans, lettuce, spinach, Chinese peas, wheat, and cherry tomatoes.

If you don't have a yard, visit a local nursery and obtain advice on raising parsley, dill, savory, and chives in a windowsill garden. Or ask their advice on planting in window boxes or bushel baskets on the deck or patio.

Make arrangements with a local grocery store to bring your children by the next time their fresh produce is to be delivered. Let the children watch the (refrigerator) truck being unloaded, the vegetables uncrated, and prepared for display. Encourage them to ask questions of the clerks. ("Why do you cut off the greenest leaves of the lettuce and throw them away? What do you do if you find a tarantula in the bananas?" ...) Finally let them each choose an item from the produce section that they'd enjoy munching on the walk or drive home. (After their selections have been purchased, see if they can tell you who chose roots to eat? Stalks? Leaves? Stems? Blossoms (fruits)? Seeds?

ENRICHMENT OBJECTS

Children's Book Day is a day dedicated to the celebration of books. Write to:

The Children's Book Council
67 Irving Place
New York, NY 10003

Ask about the available posters and materials.

The U.S. Forest Service (USDA, Washington, D.C. 20250) offers a catalog of *Forest Service Films* available on free loan from your regional Forest Service office. When ordering, be sure to keep in mind the age of the children to be seeing the films.

If you are lucky, your regional Forest Service office may be able to arrange to have Woody the Owl ("Give a hoot; don't pollute!") come and visit your children. If your area offers such a service, be sure to arrange for Woody to come—the kids will be enthralled!

APRIL EATING EXPERIENCE

Contact your local Department of Wildlife and Forestry and arrange for an expert to come and visit, and hopefully, accompany you and the kids as you learn "to stalk the wild asparagus in your area." Edible wild foods are often plentiful; they are fun to gather and taste. Because some (parts of) plants can be poisonous, you should always share this eating experience with an expert, such as a local (high school) biology or botany teacher or a park ranger. Possible food finds include wild teas, fruits, berries, dandelion greens, poke weed shoots, watercress, and nasturtium leaves and flowers!

Gather the wild foods and bring them back to school where you could prepare a wild food snack including a green salad, wild tea, and a fruit compote. (Warm cornbread would be a fine complement to the meal.) Be sure to invite the expert to stay for tea.

APRIL PUPPETS

White Glove Bunny Puppet

Collect (unmatched) white gloves (from local thrift stores). Fold the thumb across the palm of the glove and use a needle and thread to tack in place. Next, sew the fingers of the glove, middle finger with index, and ring finger with little finger, to form the bunny's ears. Use a pink felt-tip pen or a wash of light red watercolor to add the pink inside area of each ear. Sew on two buttons for eyes and a pink button nose. Use a black felt-tip pen to draw on the upper lip. A pink felt mouth can be glued beneath the lip and three pipe cleaners cut in half can be glued, or tacked with thread, to the cheeks to give the bunny whiskers. You may also add a bow tie or tie a pretty ribbon around the glove's wrist to complete the bunny puppet.

Egg Holder Finger Puppet*

Cut an egg holder from a lightweight cardboard egg carton. In the middle of one long side of the lip of the eggholder, cut out a semi-circle—this is where the finger will rest. Now set the egg holder, open side down, on the lid of the egg carton. Trace around the egg holder and cut out the traced shape. Glue it, as the back of the head, to the open side of the egg holder.

Now have the child cut two bunny ears from construction paper and glue these to the top of the head.

*Based on a puppet created by Peter Hamilton Kent and found in the February 1980 issue of *Ranger Rick Magazine*, page 15.

Tiny artificial flowers or a little bow might be glued to the top of the head also. Add two eyes, a nose, and whiskers and a mouth and your egg holder finger puppet is completed.

APRIL RECIPES

Koulourakia are the Greek Easter cookies. They are similar to shortbread with a sesame seed topping.

Koulourakia

½ cup butter
1 cup sugar (raw)
½ cup salad oil
½ cup melted margarine
⅔ cup milk

Mix these ingredients together well.

2 eggs
1 tsp vanilla

Beat these into the above mixture:

7 cups flour
3½ tsp baking powder
1 tsp salt

Sift these together and then blend into the creamed mixture to make a soft dough. Lightly flour a table-top. Give each child a piece of walnut-sized dough to roll out into a 6- to 8-inch long strand; the strand is looped in half and the right-hand half is twisted under and over the left-hand part of strand.

Place cookies on unoiled cookie sheets. Mix 2 T milk and 1 egg yolk. Brush onto cookies. Sprinkle with sesame seeds. Bake at 350° F. for 20 minutes or until golden. This makes 7 dozen cookies.

Koulitchey

Koulitchey means Resurrection Bread and it is traditionally served in Russia on Easter Day.

2 cups milk
8-10 cups whole wheat (pastry) flour
2 pkgs. yeast dissolved in ⅓ cup warm water
¼ cup corn oil

½ cup brown sugar
1 tsp salt
2 eggs, beaten well
2 cups raisins, nuts, currants
orange, lime, and/or lemon rind for decoration
cream cheese
lemon juice
whole almonds or pecans

Oil 2-4 (depending on size) coffee cans which will be used as bread pans.

Mix flour, salt, and sugar. Make a well in mixture and pour in milk mixed with dissolved yeast. Next add corn oil and eggs. Finally add nuts and raisins. Turn mixture out onto a floured tabletop and knead gently for a bit. Fill each coffee can ⅔ full with dough. Let rise in a warm spot.

Bake in the oven at 375° F. for 1 hour or until a toothpick inserted in loaf comes out clean. Allow to cool. Frost with a mixture of cream cheese and lemon juice. Use a vegetable peeler to make long strips of citrus peel. Shape these into flower petals on top of breads. Use nuts for the centers of flowers.

Finger Jell-O

3 envelopes unflavored gelatin
1 12-oz. can of frozen (grape) juice
1½ cups water

Thaw juice. Soften gelatin in it. Boil water and add the gelatin/juice mixture. Stir continually until gelatin is dissolved. (You may add honey if you like.) Refrigerate two hours or until solid.

Cut into long rectangular finger shapes. Kids love them.

MAY

… brings May flowers.

SENIOR CITIZENS MONTH

Invite several senior citizens to visit you at school. Find out some favorite food they enjoyed when they were younger. Let the children help in preparing an old-fashioned favorite food *and* one of your newer specialties. Present your guests with a pretty May basket before they leave and invite them to come and visit again soon!

MAY DAY

Although this holiday on May 1 is not celebrated as it was forty or fifty years ago, the May Day customs deserve to be revived! Explain to your children how the Pilgrims were the first to celebrate May Day in America. Pretty May baskets are made and filled with fresh flowers and cookies. Then you hang your basket on the doorknob or set it by the front door of a friend's house. Next you ring the doorbell and then you run and hide so that you may watch your friend open the door and find your basket! May baskets are a secret message of friendship and celebrate the arrival of spring!

May Baskets

Coffee Can: Punch a hole near the open end on opposite sides of the can. Glue a bright piece of paper around the can to cover its sides. Let the kids paint pretty designs on it. Insert a brad through either punched hole and attach it to the end of a tagboard strip in order to form a handle. Children may paint designs on the handle also.

Paper Doily: Fold a round doily in half. Roll it into the shape of a cone. Glue the edges down with ®Elmer's Glue-All. Allow glue to dry (or use wide tape or staples to fasten the edges together). Staple a bright colored paper handle to the top edges of basket.

Paper Plate or Bowl: Cut the plate or bowl in half across the diameter. Staple the inside facing edges together but leave the top open to form the basket's opening. Knot either end of a 14″ piece of thick pretty yarn. Staple this yarn handle to the top edges of the basket. Have the children decorate the basket with pretty stickers, glitter, and cut paper designs.

Plastic Berry Basket: Let the kids weave thin colorful strips of paper in and out of the plastic slats of the basket. Use colored cloth tape to attach an arched paper handle across the top of the basket.

Braided Paper (for older children): For each child cut 18 strips of paper ¾″ × 12″; use two or more colors. Place seven strips of one color paper in parallel rows. Take a second color strip and begin weaving in and out of rows of the first color strips. (Put aside one strip of each color to be used for handles.)

Push the woven part of strips to the middle, leaving the ends free. Now gather up the ends carefully, one strip

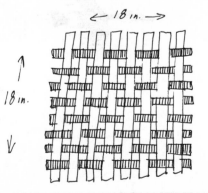

behind the other. Overlap the strip of same color which you saved for the handle and staple it in place atop the ends.

Collect the other ends and, as you did above, staple the handle where the strips cross. (See April's "Easter Baskets" for additional ideas.)

May baskets are traditionally filled with fresh flowers and some homemade cookies or pastry. If no fresh flowers are available for the children to use, you might make some of these paper flowers to place in your baskets.

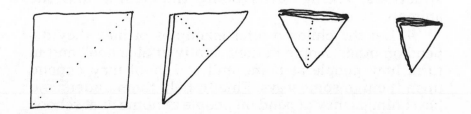

Paper Flowers

Use a square or circle of paper for each blossom. Fold the paper in half three times.

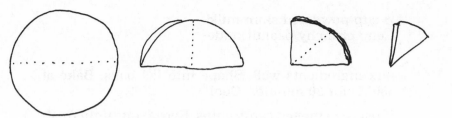

Next cut the folded paper.

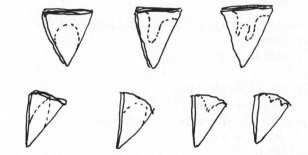

Open out the paper* and crimp together at the back of the flower, twisting a bit. Bind a green pipe cleaner to the base of the flower, forming a stem. Tie small bouquets with pretty ribbon and place in the May baskets.

May Basket Goodies

Ask the kids to think back over all the things you've baked together this year. They may choose to make their favorite recipe and use it to fill their May baskets or perhaps they would enjoy making one of the following.

Peanut Butter Mounds

2 cups graham crackers, crushed fine
½ cup brown sugar

---

*You may paste a tiny circle of contrasting color to the center of each blossom or add a spot of glue to the middle of some flowers and sprinkle with glitter.

½ cup powdered skim milk
1 cup crunchy peanut butter

Mix ingredients well. Shape into 1½" balls. Bake at 350° F. for 20 minutes. Cool.

Frost with melted carob chips. Refrigerate until frosting has hardened.

Gumdrop Cupcakes

1 lb. large gumdrops (no black ones), cut up
½ cup honey
½ cup soft butter
1 egg
¾ cup sweet applesauce
½ tsp each: cinnamon, cloves, salt
½ tsp soda dissolved in 1 T hot water
1 tsp baking powder
2 cups flour
1 cup raisins

Cream butter and honey. Add 1 cup flour, egg, baking soda, baking powder, applesauce, and seasonings.

Sift remaining cup of flour over raisins and cut-up gum drops. Mix lightly to coat each piece. Add to creamed mixture.

Spoon into cupcake holders in muffin tins; fill each holder just ½-¾ full with batter.

Bake at 350° F. for 25 minutes or until a toothpick inserted into cupcake comes out clean.

BE KIND TO ANIMALS WEEK

Explain to the kids that the first week of May is when we remember our animal friends—especially our pets—and think of how and why we can be kind and thoughtful towards them. ("They depend on us for food, water, attention, and love. They don't live out in nature any more where they could hunt for their own food and water. They give us attention and affection, so it is fair that we return it to them!")

Helping children to be able to empathize with other people *or* with animals is an important part of teaching. Here are some suggested activities to help kids learn to empathize with the animals of this world.

1. Cut out large animal pictures; identify each animal by name. Have the children imitate sounds made by that animal. Talk about what each type of sound might mean ("I'm angry, or thirsty, or afraid, or delighted, or puzzled, or hungry, or sad"). Ask them how this is similar to what *they* might say sometimes.

2. Sit in a circle. One at a time, have kids relate a possible dangerous situation in their home or out of doors ("I might fall off the back porch; I could cut myself on a piece of glass," etc.). Ask them if any *animals* could be hurt in ways like these. Finally ask them for suggestions of ways to help kids and animals to keep from getting hurt.

3. Show the kids photographs and pictures of people and pets in situations that would evoke an emotional response, such as a hungry baby crying, a pet with an empty food dish, a child being scolded, and a pet being reprimanded. Ask the children to name the feeling (emotion) being shown in each picture. Let them act out the situations, taking turns being the people and the animals.

4. Let the children offer examples of how they depend on other people in their family or at school, and in turn, how people at home and at school may depend upon them in some ways. Finally, help them understand how animals may depend on people at home or at school.

5. Help the kids to make up a few rules (laws) for taking care of a (new) school pet. Mention the best kind of behavior to have with or around this pet (and any dangerous or unkind behavior). Talk about rules for taking good care of personal pets. How do such rules (laws) help animals?

6. Demonstrate the sounds of various farm (jungle) animals (cow, pig, sheep, hen, donkey, goat, horse, monkey, leopard, bear, zebra, lion, macaw, parrot). Choose four kids to be four different farm (jungle) animal mothers* and ask them to go out of the room for a little bit. While they are gone, divide the rest of the kids into corresponding groups (or members) of baby animals. Have the four mother animals return and ask them to locate their babies by the baby animal sounds they are making. "Why would baby animals call for their parents? Why do we?"

Doggie Crackers

Let your students make the following recipe and give the crackers to their pets.

½ cup whole wheat flour	4 T lard
½ cup soy flour	½ cup water
1 cup rolled oats	½ tsp bone meal

Mix flours, bone meal, and oats. Mix lard with water and add to the dry mixture.

Roll out on a cookie sheet and bake at 350° F. until golden brown. Cool. Break into medium-sized pieces.

---

*Sometimes the animal father is the parent who cares for the young. This is true of the seahorse who incubates the eggs, the marmoset monkey who guards and nurtures his young, and the fox, wolf and coyote who bring food back to the den for the female and pups. Ninety percent of male birds are involved in some parenting.

Animal Art

Animal Pictures Made with Carbon Paper (for young kids): Place a sheet of carbon paper between two sheets of typing paper. Use a paper clip to hold these sheets together. The child uses a hard-leaded pencil to draw animal pictures on the top sheet of paper. Then he or she can lift up the carbon to see exactly the same picture as it appears on the bottom sheet. Young children are especially intrigued by this. (Try using carbons of different colors for variation.) Make certain that the youngsters understand WHY they can make two drawings at once in this way.

Animal Pictures Made with Crayon and Turpentine (for older children): The child draws an animal picture on white drawing paper using different colors of crayons. Next he or she dips a brush or cloth in turpentine and applies it to the outer edges of the drawing to achieve a misty blurred effect. **(CAUTION: Turpentine is to be used only under teacher supervision.)**

MOTHER'S DAY

Explain to the young child that the second Sunday in May is Mother's Day, the day on which we say "thank you" to our mommies for being so wonderful all year long. Ask for their suggestions for making special surprises for their mothers. Listen to and, if possible, use their ideas and then help the group to plan a treat to take home. You might use one of the ideas below or look at other gift suggestions offered throughout the *Almanack*.

Mother's Day Gifts

Scour Flower Pads (12): Buy half a yard of 48″ wide nylon net. Cut a 4″ × 18″ pattern from lightweight cardboard. Use this to trace out 12 strips from the net. Each strip is then gathered lengthwise with a (machine) running stitch and nylon thread along the middle of the net. This thread is pulled tight and tied. Finally, each flower is secured with a 10″ length of nylon string.

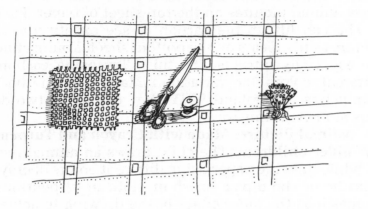

Bath Scent for the Tub (1 quart): Let the children help weigh and then fill and tie a cheesecloth bag with the following*: 1 oz. each of bay leaves, rosemary, lavender, pennyroyal, lemon peel, (dried) rose petals, (orange blossoms, if available) and table salt.

Place the bag in a pan with a quart of water. Bring the water to a boil. Simmer four minutes, cool, and strain. Use a funnel to decant the bath scent into small sterilized glass jars, one for each child. Help the kids wrap their gifts and tie the ribbons. Be sure to add a descriptive note to the gift so each mom will understand the nature of her present.

Body Rub: This after-bath rub must be made three weeks in advance, but it makes a really unique gift—one that any weary parent might appreciate. Check with a discount drugstore to find eau de cologne at a reasonable

---

*To save money, buy herbs in bulk from a co-op market or herb outlet.

price. Collect pretty little bottles with lids (or buy a selection of little corks at a hardware store), one for each child. Increase this recipe as you need to obtain the correct amount for your class:

> 2 T each: crushed rosemary
> marigold flowers

Add these to one pint of eau de cologne. Let this mixture stand for three weeks. Strain and decant into little bottles. Include a note that explains that this is a soothing body rubbing lotion.

Handmade Furniture Polish**:** Combine ¼ cup vinegar, ¼ cup turpentine, and ¼ cup *boiled* linseed oil. Decant into bottles. Print the directions to go with this polish: Shake the bottle. Rub polish on furniture with a soft cloth. Allow to stand for 20 minutes. Rub dry to a high gloss!

MEMORIAL DAY

Memorial Day is May 30, although it is observed on the last Monday in May.

Perhaps some of your children may ask what kind of holiday Memorial Day is. In such an event, you might say:

"Memorial Day used to be called Decoration Day. It was started over 100 years ago in the South of our country. There had been a terrible war when America was split in two with one part of our country fighting the other part. When it was over, sad friends and families went to put flowers on the graves of dead soldiers—of *both* sides of the war. The news of this decoration of

---

**Both turpentine and linseed oil are toxic if swallowed; for this reason it is appropriate to make *Handmade Furniture Polish* with 6-7-year-old youngsters who can understand that it must never be swallowed!

graves was heard in the North and soon all American people on this day were putting flowers on all the soldiers' graves—no matter which side they had fought on. Time passed. There were more wars and at last it was decided that *all* people who had died for our country should be remembered on this day. Memorial means 'remembered.'"

FUN WITH WIND

Making a Wind Vane: Cut two long arrows from oaktag. Place a small bottle (tiny food coloring bottle), neck down, between the arrows and glue them together. Put heavy books on either side of the bottle until the glue dries. Nail an 8″ × 22″ length of wood to a large wood block, standing upright, to a large wood block. Pound a nail* into the top of the standing piece of wood. Position the bottle on the nail. Place the wind vane outdoors; it will show you the direction from which the wind is coming.

---

*Its head should fit into neck of bottle, allowing the bottle to turn freely on it.

Wind Darts: Prepare 8-10 darts for each young child before the school day begins; older kids can make their own. Use paper drinking straws that have paper covers:

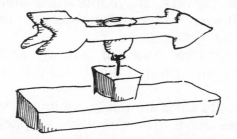

your local cafeteria or ice cream fountain shop may have some to donate to your school.

Rip open the paper top and push the paper cover down; cut off ½″ of cover as it extends below straw. Twist the end closed. Child will blow through the straw and force off the paper 'dart'. Make a target from a large piece of posterboard. Use different size holes. Have the children stand behind a given line. Let each kid try to send a wind dart through each of the target holes or give different values to the holes and let older kids keep their scores.

MAY NATURE STUDIES

Buds: The color, shape, and form of a bud is just as definite a source of plant identification as a leaf or a blossom!

Take your children on a spring walk while some of the buds on the trees and plants are not completely open. Hold down a branch so each child may see how the little group of leaves came from one bud. Let each child count the number of leaves in any bud group on the same tree. Ask the kids to each tell the number they counted. What numbers are most often said? Come back to this same tree in 2-3 weeks and see how the buds have developed.

Buds hold the beginnings of branches with their leaves and/or flowers. In plants that bloom in early spring, the flower bud is often bigger and a different shape from the leaf bud.

Often buds have waxy or gummy scales covering them. These scales protect the delicate bud and keep it moist.

The leaves of trees are really packaged in their buds. Different trees have different ways of packaging their buds. The maple leaf is folded up like a fan inside its bud. The beech leaf is packaged flat. Some leaves are folded in half crosswise and then folded in half downwards.

Try taking some large buds apart to see how the leaf within is folded. Make daily observations of a certain tree to note the leaves as they unfurl.

Try bringing some branches to school and forcing the buds to open by placing the branches in water on a sunny windowsill. The children may watch as the bud packages open. Horse chestnut, tulip tree, and beech tree buds work best. (Some buds must be frozen before opening so you had best bring in a variety of branches and this way the children can also see what type of buds require freezing before they can open.)

When examining tree buds, point out how buds always grow at the end of the branch and in the place where the leaf stem joins (joined) the branch. When a leaf falls off a tree, it leaves a scar on the twig or branch. The size and shape of the scar tells us about the size and shape of the leaf's stem. The buds that grow off the leaf scars will become next year's branches on the tree!

MAY FIELD TRIPS

Arrange to have your children visit a Senior Citizens Center or convalescent or nursing home. Have them sing several songs, give a short play* or dance or play musical (rhythm) instruments, whatever your special group of children enjoys doing. Bring along (May basket) goodies to share with the people at the center or home.

Visit a wrecking yard. Of course, make arrangements with the owners so that you do not arrive at an inopportune time. It is surprising how interesting such a place can be. Encourage the children to notice details, such as, how do you think that car got wrecked? Which one of these is older? How can you tell? How is this yard organized? Why is the wrecking yard organized in the way that it is? What parts of this car can still be used? Talk with the wreckers about their daily work. Ask questions. Get a feeling for what the job is like. What animals do the kind of work these people do? Why is such a job very important to us and to the animal world?

Have an acupuncturist visit and bring charts and needle samples. Make certain that he or she can speak in terms that the children will understand. If possible, mention the history of acupuncture. Use a globe to show where China is in relation to where you live.

ENRICHMENT OBJECTS

The *Environmental Discovery Unit on WIND* (#79043HL) is available from:

The National Wildlife Federation
1412 Sixteenth Street, N.W.
Washington, D.C. 20036

It contains background information, lesson plans, projects and add-on activities for later study and is appropri-

---

*Remember to ask the children to sing and speak loudly so that they can be easily heard by the senior citizens.

ate for use with older children. Write to N.W.F. for the price of each unit.

How about "Glow in the Dark Moons" (perhaps for the kids' bathroom?)? These are available from:

Mr. Rainbows
Department SC
P.O. Box 27056
Philadelphia, PA 19118

Ask for the current price and shipping charges.

A SPRINGTIME PICNIC

Pack a large hamper or basket, take a kite, several balls, storybooks, and go off for a springtime repast.* Here are some picnic basket-packing suggestions:

Choose from: celery sticks, olives, carrots, cherry tomatoes, cucumber rounds, and cabbage wedges.

Choose from: cheese and crackers, cream cheese and jelly sandwiches.

Choose from: grape Jell-O fingers, melon balls, fresh strawberries (and whipped cream in a plastic container with a snap lid) so kids can twirl each berry in whipped cream before eating! Of course, peanut butter cookies or carob brownies are always a treat …

Choose from: cold lemonade or … for a special end of the picnic treat in place of a dessert: Orange Sips! Roll oranges against counter top and then make a small X with point of paring knife in skin of orange. Insert a porous peppermint stick and let the kids sip their oranges!

Take a blanket or two, tissues, a thermos of water, bandages, and some meat tenderizer to use on a bee sting if—heaven forbid—such an unhappy thing should occur … and then set out and enjoy the beautiful May day!

---

*A nearby park is fine, but even your backyard can be fun!

MAY ENVIRONMENT

Collect a variety of different sizes and shapes of cardboard boxes and at least two large appliance boxes to make a railroad station and engine of the train. Cut a door and windows in the train station. Lay the boxes on their sides and cut off the tops of the boxes so that the kids can sit in them. Line the boxes up end to end. Make two holes through the end of one box and into the adjoining end of the box it touches. Thread lightweight cord through the two sets of holes and tie the boxes together. In this way secure the train cars, one to another.

Leave the cars and station undecorated. Let the children use big brushes to paint their station and train (using black for the engine and red for the caboose). Show them pictures of contemporary trains so that they can get some new ideas, too. (Plan a visit to your local train station if this is possible!)

MAY GAMES

Stop 'n Squat: Put a record on the phonograph. One child is the look-out.* Everybody else marches around the room keeping time to the music. Suddenly the music STOPS and everyone must squat! The look-out spots the last child to squat and they trade places. The game goes on.

Pyramids, a Numbers Game:** Scatter numbered paper cups (in a variety of colors) on the floor. Then ask a child to pyramid all the red cups. Next ask another kid to pyramid all the blue cups, and so on. Then ask a child to pyramid all the even-numbered cups (or odd-numbered, or cups with numbers over 5 or even-numbered pink cups, or blue cups that are less than 10). Have fun making up a variety of combinations!

---

*It should be understood that whatever the look-out says is to be obeyed right away.

**Explain beforehand what a pyramid is and how it is shaped (built).

MAY PUPPET

To make little animal finger puppets, use pinking shears to cut off the top three inches from the fingers of old brown, black, or tan gloves. Attach tiny button eyes and felt noses and mouths, and appropriate ears to make mouse, donkey, dog, or cat finger puppets.

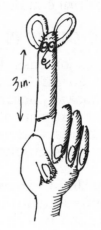

MAY RECIPES

Homemade Cheese

This procedure takes an hour or more so you might start it early and let the children have the fun of lifting out the curds as they form towards the end of the process. (The recipe makes about 2 pounds of cheese.)

4 quarts whole milk (cow or goat)
1 quart cultured buttermilk
scant tsp of salt and dill weed

Combine the milk and buttermilk in a heavy pan. Attach a candy thermometer to the edge of the pan and down into the milks. Turn on stove to medium heat. Stir once in a while to keep milk from scorching. (**NOTE:** This recipe and all recipes that require stovetop usage must always have adult supervision. An alternative method of heating liquids, etc., is to use an electric frying pan that has just a bit of water in it. Set the pot with the ingredients to be cooked into the water in the frying pan. This method allows the children to sit around the table on which the food is cooking and watch what is happening ... Thanks again, Londi.)

When the thermometer reads 170°, remove the pan from the heat until the temperature is 165°. Keep it at 165°-168° for the next hour and stir it often to keep curds from sticking on the bottom. Use a slotted spoon to remove curds and place them in a cheese-cloth-lined colander to drain. Continue this procedure until all the cheese has been collected and drained. Mix the salt and dill into the cheese to taste. Form into a flat round shape and refrigerate until cold.

(This recipe can be halved by using two quarts milk and one pint buttermilk.)

Crispy Oatmeal Crackers

¾ cup flour	¼ cup butter
¾ cup quick oatmeal	6 T cold water
¾ tsp salt	3 oz. grated (cheddar) cheese
sesame seeds	paprika

Sift flour and salt together. Cut in butter until fine crumbs form. Stir in cheese and oatmeal.

Use a tablespoon to sprinkle water onto the mixture. Stir the mixture with a fork after each addition of water.

Form dough into a ball. Flatten this out into a square, ⅛" thick. Sprinkle on seeds and press into dough.

Use a serrated knife to cut the square into 2" squares. Place these 1" apart on a cookie sheet. Bake at 425° F. for 12-15 minutes until crackers are browned. Sprinkle with paprika.

Banana Crackers

½ cup brown sugar	1¾ cup whole wheat
1 cup oil	(pastry) flour
4 eggs	(unbleached)
4 tsp baking powder	1¾ cup white flour
2 cups mashed ripe	2 tsp baking soda
bananas	2 tsp vanilla

Mix ingredients just until smooth. Pour into two buttered bread pans. Bake at 350° F. for about 1 hour or until a toothpick inserted in middle comes away clean. Cool.

Turn loaves out of pans. Use a sharp knife to cut loaves into cracker shapes. Spread these on cookie sheets and bake at 150° F. for 1 hour or until crackers are hard and crunchy.

FLORENCE NIGHTINGALE

"Florence Nightingale was born in May. She is remembered because she was so kind and helpful to the sick. We say that Florence Nightingale is the mother of modern nursing. That means she helped teach the first nurses. Today, many men are also nurses. *All* nurses have Florence Nightingale to thank for starting the profession of teaching nurses."

JUNE, JULY, and AUGUST

FATHER'S DAY

Father's Day* is the third Sunday in June.

"This is the day we say to our daddies, 'I love you, Daddy.' We make little presents to give to him, and the whole day is called 'Father's Day.' What are some reasons *you* love *your* Daddy? ... What does he do that makes you feel really happy? ... Think about how much you like him while you are drawing a picture for him on this folded paper. When your picture's finished, think of what you would like to tell him on Father's Day ... something like, 'I love you a lot,' or 'I'm glad you're my Daddy,' and I'll write it inside the card for you. Then you can sign your name."

Here is a frivolous but quite involving "Father's Day" activity for the very young: discuss "shaving" with the

kids. What is shaving? How does *your* daddy shave? Why do some men shave and other men don't? Provide the children with a can of non-mentholated shaving cream. Let them have the thrill of spraying it all over a Formica or oil-cloth covered tabletop. Then they can have the fun of playing and fingerpainting in it.

Finally, bring a plastic bucket and sponges to the table and simply swoop the foam into the bucket for an easy clean-up!

FLAG DAY

"On June 14 two hundred years ago (1777) the men who ran our country chose this flag (show a U.S. flag or at least a picture of Old Glory) to be the flag of the United States—that's the country we live in. Our flag has quite a few names. It's called the Stars and Stripes, The Star Spangled Banner, and Old Glory. How many stripes does it have? (13) There is one stripe for each of the first 'states' in our country. How many of the stripes are red? (7) How many are white? (6) Guess what those colors mean. (The red is for the blood of the people who fought to help America be a free place. The white is for a real "cleanness" in your feelings—we call that a purity in spirit— which we want to keep here in America.) There are 50 stars *now* because that's how many different states there are in America—one star for each state! Let's look outside and see if there are any flags flying ... Let's make some Stars and Stripes ourselves! Then we can put them up (outside) to show that we know today is Flag Day!"

Provide the children with crayons and white rectangles of paper or cloth (cotton sheet rectangles held by masking tape to the tabletop). Pencils and rulers and glue-backed silver stars may also be used although complete accuracy (straight lines, number of stars) is not

---

*Be especially sensitive to the feelings of kids who may be in a single-parent family or who may not have (contact with) a daddy. Such children might make a card for their grandpa if they like, or they could simply play outside for a bit while the others are finishing their cards.

essential. Then, hang the banners for passing breezes—and passersby.

THE SUMMER SOLSTICE

On June 21, or thereabouts, we celebrate the Summer Solstice. "On this day the earth is tilted so that the North Pole is as close to the sun as it ever gets. That's why today is so long; we have more hours of sunlight than on any other day. And guess what? Tonight will be the shortest night of the whole year."

THE FOURTH OF JULY

"This is the day we say, 'Happy Birthday, America!' It is the most important *American* holiday. Over two hundred years ago today (in 1776), the men who ran this land said, 'We have all decided that we want this to be a *free* country! From this day on, we will call our land, 'The United States of America!' That's why today is America's birthday and all over the country people are waving American flags and having parades to say 'Happy Birthday America!'"

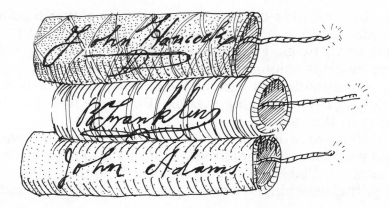

Plan a Fourth of July Parade with your kids. Use red, white, and blue crepe paper streamers, balloons, hats, flags, and banners, and parade up to the corner and back, or back and forth in your play area.

In many parts of the U.S., people go on Fourth of July picnics today. Watermelon, fried chicken, and in some places pink eggs are the traditional foods. Let the children prepare pink eggs to take on a picnic together!

Pink Eggs

Hard-boil several eggs. Cool. Shell and rinse the eggs. Place them in a bowl of juice from (a can of) pickled beets. Chill the eggs and turn occasionally as they marinate. Just before the picnic, remove the eggs from the juice and dry them on paper towels. Serve with salt—and the beets, too, if you like.

SUMMER NATURE STUDIES

Insects

Carefully catch a grasshopper. Put it in a jar. Look at it together. Ask the children to name the parts of the grasshopper: a pair of antennae, eyes that are like a crystal because they have many different sides to them, six legs, a body that has three parts to it (these are called the head, the thorax, and the abdomen), and wings. "When a creature has antennae, six legs, a body with three parts to it (and wings*), we say it is an insect.

"Now look along the side of this insect. Do you see those tiny holes? Those are the grasshopper's breathing holes. Each hole leads into a little pipe that goes all

---

*If a tiny animal has wings, it is an insect, but at some times in their lives some insects *are* wingless.

through its body to bring air to all its parts. We don't have air holes on our sides, so how do we get air all through our bodies? ... (Yes, we have lungs. Our blood gets oxygen from the air we take into our lungs. Then our blood takes the oxygen all through our bodies.)

"In the fall a lady grasshopper lays her eggs in the ground. The next spring each of these eggs will hatch and out will come a tiny grasshopper—with no wings at all. As that little grasshopper eats, it gets fatter and bigger until one day its outside shell just cracks open and there inside is a new, bigger skin. This process of shedding skin is called *molting*. The little grasshopper molts quite a few times, each time growing a bigger skin for itself. After awhile it also grows two pairs of wings— and then it is a fully grown grasshopper!

"That's the way a grasshopper grows up. Ladybugs, aphids, and beetles are born from eggs and get bigger and bigger until one day they are fully grown. Not all insects grow up in this way." Go outside and collect a butterfly in a large jar with a leafy twig from the plant it was on when you caught it. (Also put a small jarlid of water in the jar and punch plenty of air holes in the jar covering.) Be sure to release the butterfly!

"Once a grasshopper is born, it always looks like a grown-up grasshopper, only smaller. Well, once a moth or a butterfly is born, it changes its looks at different times. First the moth and butterfly are eggs. These eggs hatch and they become caterpillars. These caterpillars grow and at last they hang from a thread and cover themselves with a tight-fitting 'sleeping bag.' (The moth's bag is called a pupa, and the butterfly's bag is called a chrysalis.) Time goes by. Finally, the little sleeping bag splits open and out comes a fully grown moth or butterfly. In the beginning, its wings are all crumpled, but they soon dry in the warm sunshine and then the 'newborn' insect spreads its wings and flies away!"

Take an inventory of the very common insects near your school, such as, ladybugs, ants, flies, grasshoppers, and mosquitoes. These are the insects whose life cycles and habits you should research so that you will be able to answer any questions that may come up in school. (If you find sowbugs, millipedes, and wasps, you will need to familiarize yourself with these insects and their life patterns. A biology book from the library, such as, *Biology Made Simple* by Ethel R. Hanauer and published by Doubleday, 1972, will help you to quickly understand various insects and their life-patterns.)

An Insect Cage

Let the kids cover the bottom of a round 5-gallon commercial ice cream container with handfuls of grass and small twigs. Fill a small shallow jar lid with water and nestle it among the grass.

Go outside and carefully catch an insect (a beetle, grasshopper, or praying mantis). Place the insect on the grass in the cage.

Now roll a length of foot-wide fine mesh screening and insert it a quarter of the way down into the ice cream container. Place the open end of a 5-pound coffee can atop the screening, leaving a good eight inches of space

between the ice cream container and the coffee can. This is the finished insect cage.

Encourage the children to watch the insect and how it acts. Make a chart or pictures of what it does. Eventually put another insect in the cage with the first insect. Ask the kids to guess what will happen. Watch what happens …

An Insect Amplifier

Explain to the children that the word amplify means "to make louder." Each child will need a paper cup, a thin piece of (wax) paper, and a rubber band.

Go outside and catch a few insects. Try to have a variety (housefly, aphid, ant, ladybird, beetle, etc.). Help each child to place an insect inside a cup. Cover the mouth of the cup with the thin paper and secure it firmly in place with a rubber band. Now, the child holds the insect amplifier up to his or her ear and listens quietly … "What is your insect doing? Is it creeping, hopping, fluttering, or buzzing around?"

Seeds

"A seed is a plant's way of making a new plant. You know how a bird lays an egg and after awhile the egg cracks open and a little baby comes out. Well, a seed is a plant's egg in a way." (Take a lima bean that has been soaked in water and crack it apart.) "What do you see inside this seed? Can you see the little stem of the baby plant and the two pale leaves all folded up? When a seed is warm enough and has some water to drink, the bottom of the stem will go down into the earth and it will become the plant's root. The top of the little stem will push up out of the seed, and what do you think it turns into? The plant's stem and leaves! At first the baby plant gets its food from the seed halves that used to cover it. Then after awhile, the new leaves begin to make food for the plant and the new roots begin to bring water up into the plant. Later this plant will begin making seeds of its own!"

Help the kids name some seeds that they know (apple and watermelon, sesame, orange, grapefruit, etc.). Encourage the children to contribute to a group collection that may develop and grow throughout the summer. Perhaps you may occasionally bring in a few unusual seeds, such as, coconut, avocado, and strawberry. Help the children to split open and compare the baby plants inside several seeds: a peanut, a grapefruit seed, a pinto bean, and a maple leaf seed. "How are they all alike inside? How are they different?"

"In order to get planted, a seed needs to move from the mother plant and get to a place where it can grow. Seeds travel around in different ways. What ways have you seen seeds getting around?" (Flying: maple, dandelion, thistle; catching a ride: burrs and seeds eaten by wild birds, such as berry seeds; and buried by squirrels and other little animals: acorns.) "The coconut—the world's biggest seed—travels by water! It grows on the shores of islands with water very nearby and makes a sea voyage in order to be planted on another beach far away."

Collect many different types of seeds and try to see how each travels around.

Your children may want to plant seeds and watch them as they grow.* (Try lettuce, radishes or dwarf marigolds—all of which are rapid growers!) Often the kids will ask if the seeds they collect themselves will grow if they plant them. Explain how different seeds have different needs. Some seeds must rest for several months before they can grow. Some seeds must have their outer shells cracked. Some seeds have to be frozen before they can sprout. But go ahead and try planting the seeds found nearby. Keep track of your results.

Get a good tree field guide. It will tell you about the trees in *your* area.

(In August help the youngsters make Squirrel Food. Wash watermelon seeds. Place them on a baking sheet. Put into a 225° F. oven for half an hour. Stir the seeds every ten minutes. Cool the seeds and then take them to an area where squirrels live. Sprinkle the seeds about. Return the following day. What do the children see? (footprints and fewer seeds)

SUMMER NATURE WALKS

Go for a walk early in the morning (or just after a rainfall). Bring along a pair of hand lenses. Ask the children: "How does it smell outside today?" Close your eyes: "What special summer sounds do you hear?" Walk further and ask, "How are the things we see and smell different today, different from things we saw and felt in the winter? (or even way back last fall)"

As you walk along, keep a watch for the biggest (furriest, greenest, noisiest, most beautiful) tree (dandelion, bird, leaf, plant, bush).

At one point choose a child who volunteers "to shut his or her eyes tight and keep them closed." Let the other children hand this child different things from nature: a smooth rock, two very different types of leaves, pine needles, and pieces of bark, and ask the child to describe the feeling of each of these natural textures. Later, other children may want to play this guessing game.

While on your walk make a tape recording of sounds heard outdoors, such as, bird songs, rustling leaves, crunching of dried grasses or pebbles, snapping of twigs, rushing water, traffic sounds, footsteps on the sidewalk, barking of dogs. Once you are back at school play the tape back for the children and have them identify (and re-experience) their nature walk in the summer.

SUMMER ART PROJECTS

Stick Prints

Collect a wide assortment of wooden sticks: pencils, dowels, clothespins, chopsticks, spools, match sticks, and cotton swabs. The child dips the end or the side of a stick into a flat container of slightly thickened poster paint. Then he or she presses the stick onto a (newspaper padded) sheet of paper. This procedure is repeated over and over again as the child forms an all-over pattern of stick prints.

Children may experiment with creating borders, making set patterns, or using two colors of paint, alternating the light and the dark, the end(s) and the side(s) of stick(s). This can be a very soothing activity on a summer afternoon.

---

*Also sprout birdseed. Wet a paper towel and sprinkle it with seeds. Fold up the towel and place it in a drinking glass that always has a small amount of water in the bottom just touching the towel. Keep a chart to show how much each kind of seed grows.

Foil Painting

Make a mixture of liquid detergent and tempera paint. Use strips of masking tape to hold large pieces of foil to the tabletop. Have the child paint directly onto the foil. These paintings are quite magical in appearance. Rainbows, butterflies, birds, flowers, fairies, and designs all make suitable subjects.

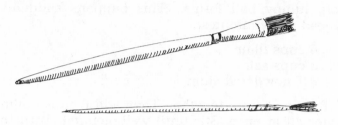

Rice Designs

The child drips white glue onto a piece of colored paper. Next he or she sprinkles grains of rice onto the wet glue. The paper is set aside and the glue is allowed to dry. Finally, the paper is tilted so that any unglued kernels will slide off the paper. The child may use felt-tip pens or tempera paints to add color to this rice design, if desired. (Salt, sawdust or cornmeal could be used instead of rice.)

Stringing Beads (for older children)

Spread out a blanket under a shade tree or other shady area and spend the afternoon stringing beads and making necklaces. Provide the kids with lengths of string, each with a button tied to the end. If needles are used, double the string to prevent it from slipping out of the needle. Provide a variety of things to string: dyed* pasta or rice, seeds (watermelon, corn, canteloupe, and black-eyed peas softened in water), buttons, little styrofoam packing shapes, small paper shapes with paper-punched holes, corn starch beads, and easy-to-hold plastic and glass beads with holes that are simple to thread. (Very young children may put beads into their mouths or ears, so this activity may be inappropriate for them.)

Corn Starch Beads. Mix ¾ cup flour, ½ cup corn starch, and ½ cup salt in a bowl. Add warm water until mixture can be kneaded into a stiff dough. Dust the children's hands with flour to prevent them from sticking to the dough. Kids can shape beads into many different forms. Pierce each with a round toothpick. Allow to slowly dry. Beads are painted with poster paint. When paint is dry, glue may be brushed on and glitter sprinkled over beads.

Old Crayon Pictures

Peel off the paper covers from used, broken crayons. Scratch and cut grooves, lines, and notches into the sides of the crayons. Let the kids rub the crayons flatwise across their papers to achieve patterns, designs, and stylized pictures.

Textured Prints

Each child uses a wide brush and slightly thickened tempera paint to coat a textured cloth (net, burlap, monk's cloth) or paper, corrugated cardboard, or styrofoam packing pieces. Next, the child lays a piece of newsprint over the painted area and presses down on it, lightly rubbing the paper's surface. When the paper is lifted up, a textured print appears.

---

*To dye pasta or rice, place ¼ cup rubbing alcohol and a large amount of food coloring in a pint jar. Add pasta or rice. Shake until pasta or rice is the right color. Dry immediately in a wire sieve or on a paper towel-lined cookie sheet.

Kids may overlap printed areas and use different colors of paint to obtain variations on their textured prints.

Fingerpaint

Here's *another* recipe for this all-time favorite art material! Mix 3 T cornstarch with 3 T cold water. Add one cup boiling water and stir constantly until mixture is of a fingerpaint consistency. Add a squirt of liquid detergent to the mixture. Sift powdered tempera paint (or add liquid tempera directly) into the cornstarch mixture. Child uses fingerpaint on the glossy side of meat market (freezer wrap) paper or paints a cookie sheet with hands or decorates pages of a wallpaper sample book.

Sawdust Clay

    2 cups sawdust (not redwood)
    1 cup flour
    1 tsp salt
    1-2 cups water

Add water to dry ingredients to achieve a clay-like consistency. Child may pat out clay into a small slab and then press leaves or shells into it to produce a design, landscape or figure. Child makes a small round hole near top of slab and allows clay to dry before hanging up this sawdust clay picture.

Homemade Play Clay

There are many variations to this Play Clay recipe. Try the following and decide which one you prefer.

    1. 1 cup flour
        ½ cup salt
        2 tsp cream of tartar
        1 cup water

        1 T oil
        1 tsp food coloring
    2. 3 cups flour
        1 cup salt
        1 to 1½ cups water
        ¼ cup cooking oil

For recipes 1 and 2, use a non-stick pot. Stir ingredients together well. Heat over medium heat until a soft, lumpy ball forms. (This happens suddenly.) Knead a few minutes.

    3. 6 cups flour
        3 cups salt
        3 T powdered alum

For recipe 3, mix together. Then add 6 cups boiling water all at once. Stir until well-blended. Turn the dough out onto a thick pad of newspaper topped with wax paper. Allow to cool for 10 minutes. Now add 1 T salad oil. Divide dough into 6 pieces. Knead 7 minutes. Add coloring.

Play clay should last four months if it is wrapped tightly in plastic wrap and then in a close-sealed plastic bag and kept in the refrigerator.

Collage (for very young kids)

Child rubs a few drops of baby oil onto wax paper and presses torn colored tissue onto it. A few more drops of oil are then added to surface and a second layer of tissue may be applied.

Collage (for older kids)

Colored tissue paper is cut and torn into different shapes. Children use brushes to apply liquid starch onto heavy paper. Next they lay tissues on the papers. Allow collages to dry.

A coat of diluted white glue can be painted onto the collages to give them glossy surfaces. (Finally, details may be added to dried surfaces by using a felt-tip pen, crayon, or poster paint.)

The Big Crazy Crayon Machine

Each child chooses 3-7 crayons to be used to make his or her own crazy crayon machine. Wide masking tape is used to bind crayons together, with their points all on one level.

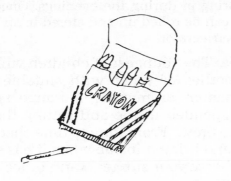

Big sheets of paper are provided and kids are asked to use their machines to draw BIG on these papers.

Paper Mosaics

Child draws a (large) design outline on a piece of white paper. Next he or she arranges pre-cut 1″ squares of

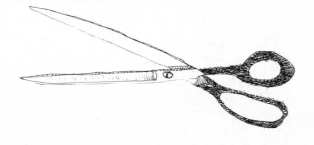

paper within the outline, leaving a little space in between each paper. These squares are glued in place once the colors/arrangement are satisfactory to the artist.

Painting Variation Possibilities

Let the kids try painting with feathers, notched cardboard pieces, corncobs, or corks.

Whipped Paint Pictures: These can be made by combining a 12-oz. box of cold water starch and an equal amount of soap flakes. Whip this mixture with a rotary egg beater (or electric beater). Add poster paint for color.

A variation on this can be made by combining soap powder and a bit of water to form a smooth paste. Dry poster paint is added and this is whipped until it becomes stiff.

Pictures from Geometric Shapes

(This activity is for the very young.) Use different colors of paper and cut a dozen each (ranging from one to four inches) of the following shapes: circle, rectangle, triangle, square. Encourage the kids to play with several of these shapes by moving them about on a piece of (white) paper, forming landscapes, houses or people. Have them glue the geometric shapes in place. Display a group of these pictures together so that the children can see the many different ways in which the shapes were used.

SUMMER NATURE PROJECTS

Sun Fun

"The sun is really a star. It is our closest star. The sun is a very very big ball of burning gases. It is *so* hot that it glows with a fierce bright light. The sun's light can give you a suntan, but if you aren't careful it may also burn you. Never look straight at the sun because its light can burn your eyes, too.

"All living things need the sun. Green plants use sunlight to make their food. Animals eat plants or other animals that eat plants. We use the sun's light and heat every day. We could not live for long without our sun."

Sunshine Prints: Each child will need a small rectangle of glass and a piece of studio proof or printout paper available at camera shops. (Cut the paper to fit each pane of glass. Do this indoors and out of light.) Offer the children a variety of small flat objects and help them find others out of doors (feathers, leaves, string, paper doilies, coins, buttons, pieces of lace, pressed flowers or butterflies, paper cutouts).

Each child arranges objects on his or her paper (which is itself placed on a magazine to facilitate later transportation). Next the glass is laid on top of the paper and the magazine with glass-covered paper is moved into the sun. Leave them in the sun until the paper has turned very dark. Then bring them indoors. Remove the glass and the objects. Let the kids admire one another's sunshine prints. (These prints will slowly fade. Keep them out of sunlight or treat them chemically to set the prints if you like. Inquire about treatment chemicals at the camera shop as you purchase the paper.)

Sundried Fruit Leather: If you live in an area that has lots of sunshine and/or dry air, you can make fruit leather out of doors. If, however, your climate is humid, simply place the cookie sheet overnight in a 150° F. oven of a gas stove—either drying technique will give your children a nutritious, chewy snack!

> 4 cups fresh fruit (apricots, strawberries, cherries, etc.—experiment!), washed and pitted
> ¼ cup sugar

Combine fruit and sugar (and heat to 180° F.). Puree in a blender. Pour out onto plastic-wrap covered cookie sheets. Make certain that the puree is spread evenly to ¼″ thickness. Place out of doors in the sun for 2 days. Bring in during the evenings. Once dry, fruit leather can be rolled up and stored in an airtight jar in the refrigerator.

Sun Tea: The youngest of children will enjoy preparing large bottles of water with suitable herb teabags (apple cinnamon or mandarin orange spice are good choices) suspended inside and setting these out in the sunshine "to brew." From time to time check the coloring of your tea and bring it inside when it has steeped to suit your taste. Serve your sun tea warm or ice cold and sip it together outside.

Sundried Fruits and Vegetables: Older children will be able to (pare and) slice apples, apricots, peaches, carrots, zucchini, and celery. Use a large blunt-nosed needle and heavy thread to pierce and string each piece. Leave air spaces between the pieces. Do not dry in direct sunlight as it may make apricots bitter.

Fruits dried in this way will keep for months and are wonderful for snacks, either with plain yogurt or by themselves. The vegetables can also be stored until some chilly autumn day when the children toss them into chicken broth for a warming soup snack!

Fun with Shadows, Clouds and Rainbows: "It is because of the sun that we have shadows, clouds, and rainbows!"

Capitalize on sunny summer days. Help the kids make and play with shadows made with their hands, objects, and moving things. Look at clouds long and often. Find shapes that look like the beginning of a story. Tell it. Then look for another cloud figure that gives you an idea for how to continue the story. Use the garden hose or a gentle sprinkler to make rainbows on the next sunny day. Experiment with stopping and starting the rainbows. Can the kids figure out why they are able to do this? Bring a (few) crystal(s) to school. Twirl them in the sunlight. "It looks so lovely and magical. Do you know why crystals can make little rainbows?" (Sunlight looks clear and yet it has all colors in it. The lines of light that come down from the sun are called rays. When the sun's rays hit the many sides of the crystal, the rays bend and show all the colors that there are. We usually don't see all the colors because the sun's rays usually just hit flat sides. But because a crystal (and a prism) have more than one flat side, they break up the sun's rays and make them show all the colors there are in sunlight!)

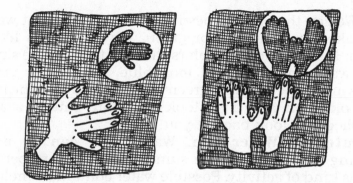

Water Fun

"All living things on earth need water in order to keep on living.

"You can't taste water. You can't smell water and it doesn't have any color.

"Water is made of two gases: one is called hydrogen and is a very light gas, and the other is called oxygen. When hydrogen and oxygen get together in a certain way you get water!

"Water can look three different ways: it can be wet and running out of a faucet or out of a glass when you drink it. Water can be hard and cold when it's an ice cube or an icicle. When you boil water to make a cup of tea, what comes out of the spout of the teakettle? Steam? Right! And what is steam? Just another shape that water can take.

"Have you ever wondered what happens to the puddles after it rains? The sun comes out and shines on the puddles and pretty soon the puddles are all gone! Well, the sun heated some of the water and made it go up into the air—it evaporated—like the steam from a boiling teakettle. Some of the water in the puddle probably sank down into the ground to bring the tree and plant roots a drink!

"We say that water doesn't have any color, but water in a lake can look blue or green. Why? Water is like a mirror. It gives back the colors that hit it. When the sky is blue, water in a lake will look blue, too. If tiny green plants are in the water, or green trees are above it, the lake will look green. And if you look down into water in a lake, your face will look back at you!"

Outdoors Water Fun: Water play can be both soothing and sensual. The summer months are perfect for this kind of activity. Possible water containers include plastic tubs, aluminum tubs, wading pools.

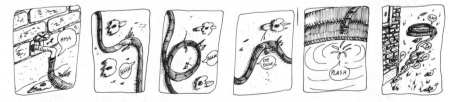

Before you introduce the kids to the water fun, consider what rules you may want to have to insure everyone's safety and peace of mind: use the towels before you go back inside; don't put food or clothes in the water; and please don't throw the water.

Really keep a low profile. Let the children enjoy themselves with little, if any, adult intervention. Simply show them the wading pool and lots of plastic or metal toys, utensils (supply just a few of these each time they play: small sponges, squeeze and pill bottles, funnels, measuring cups, spoons, a tea strainer, eye-droppers, clear plastic tubing, tin pie pans and lids, small wooden blocks and styrofoam cups, a few packing chips, and corks) and then let them enjoy. The kids may:

- pour water from one container to another (through a funnel or tube)
- give their dolls baths and shampoo their hair
- make boats and rafts, experimenting with what can float and what won't float
- have fun with the bottom half of plastic detergent bottles into which you have pierced holes of different sizes (use a heated metal knitting needle or shishkabob skewer to make the holes)
- play with spray bottles that give off soft mists rather than hard sprays
- try to figure out what are the best shapes for floating and what kinds of things never will float (help them experiment with foil: flatten, fold, bend, and overlap it to see what shapes float well)
- wash out handkerchiefs, small scarves, and cloth napkins and hang them up to dry

Two Boats to Make: A *soap-powered raft* is cut from a waxed milk carton. Use a hole punch to make an indentation near the rear of the raft. Child gently places the raft on water's surface. Then he or she drops a little liquid soap into the indentation and watches the raft being self-propelled!

Kids glue and insert one paddle into the other.

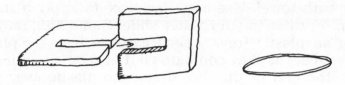

They glue the wheel (little spool) and captain (big spool) in place.

Next they place a thick rubber band over the paddle and insert it into the back of the boat. Stretch the rubber band so that each side fits into a groove.

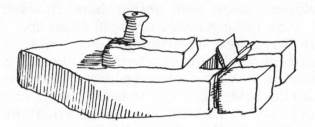

Finally, the paddle is twisted backwards several times and held in place as the "Robert E. Lee" is set upon the waters of the Mississippi!

Young children will enjoy constructing simple boats from plastic margarine tubs, styrofoam meat trays, and corks of different sizes. Provide them with a variety of lightweight materials and let them experiment to learn for themselves what materials make the best boats—and why.

A Water Slide: Purchase six yards of heavy plastic (a plastic hall runner or plastic sheeting from a fabric store). Position the plastic down a small hill or if you have a smooth-surfaced door that comes off its hinges, you can tilt this at a slight angle and cover it with the plastic. Hold the plastic in place with large cement blocks. Cover each

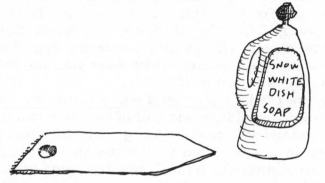

A *Mississippi riverboat* is precut from wood and the kids have the fun of assembling and operating it.

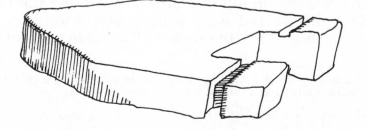

block with thick padding, such as a small throw rug or heavy bath towel. Use a garden hose to apply a steady stream of water to your water slide! Some kids may try sitting on plastic trays, heavy garbage bags, or plastic snow-saucers as they come down. Let them experiment.

At the end of the day, drape the plastic over your clothesline and let it dry.

A heavy duty plastic wading pool is excellent for kids to use for outdoor water play. If such a pool is impractical for you, cut a large tire in half crosswise and create two donut shaped pools for very young children.

Indoors Water Fun: Tape garbage bags flat beneath the children's work area and/or have sponges and a bucket ready for any necessary spill clean-up.

Clay Dams and Reservoirs: Let the older children use plasticene modelling clay to make into long coils and then construct water reservoirs, dams, and causeways. They should have fun experimenting with channeling water and playing with the concept of irrigation.

More Ways to Have Fun with Water: Give the children wide paintbrushes (or sponges) and buckets (or coffee cans) of water for hours of fun 'painting' the sidewalk, fence, the side of your building, or outdoor furniture.

Ask the children to tell you some things they know about water. "Water is clear and I can see through it; water is in lakes and ponds and rivers and the ocean; water can make rain (snow, sleet, hail). You can freeze it into ice cubes or boil it for tea."

Help the kids, as a group, to write *The True Life Story of a Raindrop (or a Snowflake)*. Let them make drawings to illustrate each important part of this biography.

Make a big mural to show lots of different ways and places that water is found.

Make a long list together: name all the different ways you used water yesterday! Older children may enjoy developing a simple bar graph from the facts in this list.

Go through old magazines and find pictures of water in different forms. Divide the pictures into three groups: water used for food, for work, and for play. Now paste the water pictures onto a big piece of paper so that these divisions are clearly shown.

Let the children have fun acting out these water-oriented situations: "Pretend you are a little stick laying on the ground. It begins to rain. It rains real *hard*. Show what happens to you. At last it stops raining. Show what happens to you *then*." Or, "You are a raindrop falling from the clouds. First you land in a puddle and then you become part of a stream. Show how this feels. Show where you go." Or "You are water in a faucet. Someone turns you on and you go into a watering can. They use you to water their plants. Show how you like this and what happens to you next."

Purchase a long-stemmed white carnation. Split its stem lengthwise. Place one half of the stem in a glass of water dyed red with food coloring. Place the other half of the stem in a glass filled with water that is dyed blue. Have the children watch the flower. How long does it take for the blossom to show that the water has reached it?

"Water really has an invisible skin.* That's why some little insects can skate right across water. They are so light that they don't sink. We can drop a double-edged razor blade flat on top of a dish of water and the razor blade will float. But what will happen if we drop the blade sideways onto the water? (The blade will cut the

---

*You can see this skin when you fill a glass slowly right up to its top. The water will actually bulge a tiny bit over the edge of the glass!

water's invisible skin and then the blade will fall to the bottom of the glass.)"

Pour some pepper on the water in another glass. The pepper floats. Put your finger in the water and the pepper keeps on floating. But now put a little drop of liquid dishwashing soap into the water. Why did the pepper speed away? (The oil in the soap changed the water's skin and pushed the pepper away!)

Sand Play

If it is practical in your school space, consider inflating a large wading pool* and filling it with soft clean (white building) sand. Little kids will spend hours making molded shapes by packing wet sand in tuna cans, yogurt containers, and frozen juice cartons. Older kids will enjoy using such shapes in combination to construct buildings, castles, towns, trains, dragons, or sea-serpents. Be sure to provide a variety of objects to be used as ornamental devices including feathers, short wooden dowels, bottle caps, or short lengths of cord.

Such sand play as is afforded by a wading pool or sandbox is very comforting, especially on days when it's too cold or wet to have fun outside.

Rocks Inside Our School

The children should have lots of fun looking for and discovering examples of rocks and minerals that are all around them right in their school room. First look around your school yourself and list the types of rock and rock derivatives you are able to locate. Then check yourself against the following list. How well did you do?

---

*You may want to spread out a blanket or plastic sheet on which to set the pool, and to catch any overflow of sand during the children's play.

- Building materials (bricks, mortar, slate, field rock (fireplace), flagstone, tile, concrete, cement, and plasterboard)
- Plaster of paris
- Blackboard chalk (gypsum)
- Pottery includes earthenware (such as rusty red flowerpots, stoneware, chinaware)
- Writing pencils
- Baby powder
- Sandpaper and emery boards

Be certain that the children understand what rocks and stones are and discuss with them how they are like and unlike the more grownup sounding "minerals." (" *Minerals* are made by nature. They are never alive like plants and animals. Minerals are found in the ground. There are many different kinds of minerals and each one has a name. Coal is a mineral. So are quartz and mica. Aluminum, nickel, iron, and diamonds are all minerals, too. Now a *rock* is made when different kinds of minerals get squeezed together. Sometimes heat and water also work on the minerals and help change them into a rock. Guess what a *stone* is? Just a small piece of a rock!)

SUMMERTIME FIELD TRIPS

Use the Yellow Pages of your phone book to give you ideas for local field trips that you and the children might take. Consider the current interests and the personalities of your kids when selecting these trip locales. Energetic kids would probably enjoy visiting a crane and winch company, the airport, a trout farm, a brickmaking company, a water processing plant, a foundry, a road under construction, and a railroad roundhouse. Children who enjoy quietly watching a process will have fun at a beauty shop, a tofu-making plant, a woodworking shop, an aikido demonstration, an armored car, or an ambulance service. If large billboards are used in your community, arrange with the outdoor advertising company to take older children to watch the changing of a local billboard—it's quite surreal to see the huge images overlapping one another.

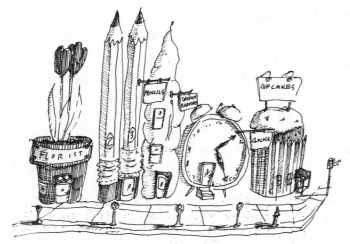

You can arrange to take a trip and visit a large (community) garden. If possible, have the kids pick green beans. Take the beans back to school and wash and

split them halfway up. Once dried, these beans become the leather britches that pioneer women used in winter soups … now you may, too!

Go to a local ice cream shop early in the morning and watch ice cream being made. Contact the shop owners well in advance and arrange to bring the children at a time that is convenient for the ice cream makers. Have an extra parent along so that some kids may, when they grow restless, go outside and wait for the rest of the kids. (Be prepared to buy a small cone for each child as a finale to this trip; often the shop owner will offer complimentary cones, which is a pleasant surprise—but in all events, bring along paper napkins or tissues for the walk or ride back. There will very likely be a spill.)

That's seventeen field trip ideas—more than enough for each week of summer. You may find more regional suggestions by contacting the reference librarian of your local library.

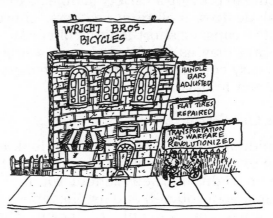

ENRICHMENT OBJECTS

The National Forest Service offers excellent wildlife posters of common flowers and trees. Secure two copies of the leaf poster and cut it into squares, one leaf to each square. Introduce the children gradually to the various leaf shapes*, beginning with very unlike shapes, such as American Elm and the White Oak, and the Redwood. Next play a little game of Concentration using just these six cards: 2 elm, 2 oak, and 2 redwood. All cards are face down on the table. The first player turns up two cards, trying for a match and naming leaves on the cards as they are turned up. If he or she succeeds, that player gets another turn. If he or she does not turn up a pair, he or she replaces the cards face down and a second player tries to turn over a pair. Soon older children will be able to quickly name all twelve leaf forms from the chart.

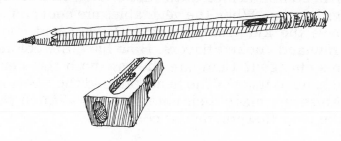

These charts, as well as charts of flowers, fish, birds, animals, and butterflies, are available from:

The Forest Service Office of Information
517 Gold Avenue, S.W.
Albuquerque, NM 87102

SUMMERTIME EATING EXPERIENCES

An Ice Cream (or Frozen Yogurt) Social

Help the kids prepare three different kinds of homemade ice cream or frozen yogurt. Do this early in the day and then bring it out of the freezer the last half hour. Let them sample all three kinds. Talk about how they are different. Which tastes best? Why? Why do some of us prefer one kind, while others like another kind? Encourage the children to use many different words to describe the frozen treats and then share the ice cream with parents as they arrive!

Homemade Ice Cream

1 cup powdered sugar
4 cups whipping cream
¼ tsp salt
4 egg whites
2 T vanilla

Whip the cream until it is stiff. Add the sugar by passing it through a sifter. Add the vanilla. Mix well. Add the salt to the egg whites and beat until very stiff. Fold the egg whites into the whipped cream mixture. Pour this mixture into refrigerator trays and freeze. This makes 16 servings.

Whole Egg Ice Cream

8 eggs, separated
2 cups cream
scant ½ cup powdered sugar, sifted
flavoring of your choice

Beat the egg whites until stiff. Beat the cream until stiff. Add the whites to the cream.

Mix the egg yolks with the sugar. Combine the cream mixture with the sugar mixture. Finally stir in your flavoring. (Take a vote as to what flavoring the majority would like; you may use flavoring extract, such as banana, strawberry, or peppermint, or sift in carob or cocoa powder to desired strength.)

---

*Certainly select leaves from local trees with which the children may already be familiar.

Place the mixture in freezer trays and freeze for one hour. Remove the trays and empty the contents into a big bowl. Beat thoroughly. Return the mixture to trays and freeze once again. This makes 16 servings.

Strawberry Sherbet

Soak 4 tsp gelatin in ½ cup cold water. Purée and then strain 2 quarts of strawberries. Add 8 T lemon juice to the berries.

Now boil 3½ cups water and 1½ cups sugar for 10 minutes. Dissolve the gelatin in the hot sugar water. Cool. Then add berries. Chill this mixture. Fold into it 4 stiffly beaten egg whites and ¼ tsp salt.

Pour the sherbet into a freezer tray. Freeze the sherbet 4 hours or more. Every ½ hour stir the sherbet from back to front. Finally beat it with electric beater just before serving. This makes 10 servings.

Frozen Yogurt Popsicles

Mix 1 quart plain yogurt with ½ tsp vanilla and one 6-ounce can of undiluted fruit juice. Spoon the mixture into paper cups and stand a wooden stick upright into each cup. Freeze. They are delicious.

FLOWERS GOOD ENOUGH TO EAT

Take a short walk with the children. Go to a park or garden where the kids may examine some small flowers, such as dandelions or clover.

Once the children have each had a chance to look closely at a flower, talk a bit about what a flower is. (A flower is the part of a plant that makes pollen and/or seeds.) Find an example of pollen (and immature seeds) on the flowers you are examining.

Ask the children if people ever eat flowers. Then tell them that they are going to have three kinds of flowers (broccoli, cauliflower, (candied) violets, nasturtiums, and dandelions are all edible flowers) to eat for snack today!

"Cauliflower is really a lot of very young flowers all closely packed together. Broccoli and very young ears of corn are also flowers! Let's look real close at these cauliflower and broccoli. Can you see the tiny flowers? Now let's wash them and break them apart into little flowers or florets. Try tasting them. What do you think? They're kind of refreshing."

Cut off the lower ½-inch of each broccoli floret. Place the vegetables in a steamer (save a few raw ones) and steam 15-20 minutes or until just tender. Brush vegetables with butter. When the vegetables are cool enough to eat, have the kids sample these flowers and compare their raw and cooked flavors. How have the colors and textures changed? Compare the raw with the steamed. What changed them? (The heat softened the fibers in the vegetables and made their colors deeper.) Which way do you like *your* flowers: raw or cooked?

The Leaning Towers of Carrots

Here is another warm day snack that is as much fun to prepare as it is to consume. Provide very young children with carrots sliced into rounds. Let each child spread peanut butter on a carrot round and adhere it to the next carrot, in this way forming a funny carrot tower. Encourage the kids to count the carrot rounds in their individual towers. You may add little toothpick flags to crown each tower and announce the end of construction—and the beginning of consumption!

Later have the children go through magazines and cut out pictures to illustrate a chart of *Things We Eat.*

Make a long list of foods the children eat, and be sure to include water. Once the chart and list are complete, ask the kids to look them over and say which foods come from plants. Next ask them which foods come from animals, and, finally, what do these *animals* eat … ?

Go to a local grocery store (with three or four kids at a time) and list all the foods that come from trees, plants, and bushes. When you get back to school, make pictures that show *Where Plants Get Their Food* (sun, earth, water, air).

Finally, help the kids prepare fresh juice. Set up a juice stand in front of the school and sell cups of cold juice to passersby!

COOKING AND EATING OUTDOORS

Snacks never seem as tasty as when you prepare and eat them outside. This summer try preparing some of these recipes out of doors with your youngsters.

Spread a plastic tablecloth on a shady piece of ground. Use two plastic or metal mixing bowls. (Have

paper towels handy and a wet washcloth in a plastic bag to facilitate clean-up. Bring a big brown paper bag to carry back any throw-aways.) Provide the children with

table knives, a large cutting board, and washed carrots, celery, cauliflower, and green peppers. Once the vegetables are cut into manageable pieces, place them in one bowl. In the second bowl, have the children prepare one of these dip recipes.

Sunflower Dip

1 cup yogurt
½ cup sunflower seeds, roasted and ground
¼ cup chives
½ tsp sea salt

Blend the above ingredients and enjoy as a dip with fresh raw vegetables or crackers.

Asparagus Dip

2 cans asparagus (broken pieces), drained and pureed
1 cup celery, diced
1 tsp sea salt
3 T lemon juice
1 tsp commercial herb mix containing parsley, shallots, salt, pepper, basil, marjoram, and celery salt

Mix the ingredients and then enjoy with fresh raw vegetables or crackers.

Fruit Fondue

Before you go outside, prepare the fruits and whip the cream. Carry these to your snack spot and sit on a big plastic tablecloth while you share your fruit-filled melon basket. Cut around a watermelon's (or honeydew's or cantaloupe's) circumference in zigzag fashion and then clean out the seeds. Scoop out the melon to form a well. Make small chunks of the melon that you extract. Cut grapes, apples, bananas, oranges, and peaches into small cubes. Fill the melon basket with a variety of these fruit cubes. Add a few tiny sprigs of mint for flavor and color. (You might also add a little lemon juice to the fruit mixture to prevent browning.)

Provide the children with sturdy toothpicks or fondue forks and a large wide-mouthed flat container of whipped cream. The children can select fruit cubes, spear them, and either dip them into the whipped cream or pop them into their mouths.

SUMMERTIME ENVIRONMENTS

(These suggestions might be used either indoors or outside, as your children prefer.)

A Den: Discuss what a den is (a hiding place, such as a cave), which animals use dens (bears, foxes, lions), and how they prepare their dens (by tramping down the grass, finding a safe hole in which to hide). Then provide the kids with soft pillows, blankets, small rugs, and large cardboard boxes. Ask them to make a den or two in which they can hide, or play bears or lions!

A Nest: Discuss "a nest" (a cozy, safe place in which to live or rest, lay eggs and protect and rear your babies).

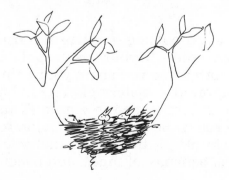

Continue the discussion as discribed above in "A Den." Give the children soft blankets for indoors, or help them collect dried grass, leaves, and sticks to make a nest to play in outside.

A Doghouse: If your very young children would enjoy playing Mother Dog and her Puppies, you may provide them with a large (drier or washer) appliance box, soft blankets for inside, and large shallow dishes of water and dried food (breakfast cereal).

Another Planet: During these summer months, the children will appreciate having an entirely different alternative environment in which to play from time to time. The landscape of another planet can be produced either outdoors or inside the school. You may set it up one evening after school in preparation for (arrival of very young children) the next day, or you can offer the kids a variety of building components and let them help to construct their own outer-space play area.

A short discussion about how it looks on the moon accompanied by vivid book illustrations can be a good lead-up to the group construction.

Look around your home (garage or basement), your school, and the disposal bins of a large department store and collect boxes, small pieces of furniture or display units, fabric lengths, packing materials, a lamp or two, Mylar pieces, a hammock, soft screening, blankets, pillows, and hardy potted plants. These should be assembled so as to offer tunnels, dark areas, hide-outs and unexpected touches such as a blinking light, a (safely hung) mirror, a tape recorded voice, and a small "outdoor space scene" lit from behind.

Encourage the children to play different roles within this other-world environment: robots, explorers, astronauts, and the people or creatures from that other planet.

HOMEMADE STILTS

Each child will need two large metal juice cans, can opener and two lengths of (clothesline) rope in order to construct a pair of stilts.

Use the can opener to make two holes equi-distant from one another and just beneath the unopened lid of each can.

One length of rope is threaded through the two holes of each can.

At this point the child stands, one foot on each can, and pulls up on the two ropes. The ends of each rope are then knotted into a loop at a convenient height for the child. Now the child pulls on the rope of the right can as he or she moves that foot, and next on the rope of the left

can. You then have tin can stilts in action! (Be certain that these stilts are used on a grassy smooth area, rather than over rocky terrain.)

SUMMER PUPPET

Make a body puppet in which the child becomes the puppet! Each child will need a lightweight cardboard box (12″ × 24″ or 24″ × 30″). The first body puppets may all be ponies and horses. If your children really love these puppets, you may later want to vary the construction and produce other animals, birds, airplanes, or fish!

For each puppet, remove the bottom of the cardboard box. Center a hole in the top of the box. The child's torso should comfortably fit into this space. In the middle of each side, an inch or two down from the top, cut a rectangular hole. The child holds the puppet body up by the two handles. Staple the horse heads to the front of each body and horse tails (yarn or rope or crepe paper) to the rear of each. Let the kids paint their body puppets, adding spots, saddle cinches, blankets, manes, and faces. Once dry, the horse puppets are put into action! See if the kids, after a while, are interested in creating a play with these puppets.

SUMMER RECIPES

No-Bake Sesame Cookies

½ cup honey
½ cup creamy peanut butter
½ cup unsweetened coconut
1 cup powdered milk
1 cup sesame seeds

Heat honey and peanut butter until melted. Add the rest of the ingredients. Pour into an 8″ × 8″ pan. Pat down into the pan. Refrigerate. Cut into squares to serve.

Hearty Southwestern Pan Bread

1½ cups cooked black or kidney beans
¾ cup juice from beans
(1 onion chopped fine)
(1 garlic clove, minced)
(1 tsp chili powder)
½ tsp cumin
½ tsp salt
¼ cup fresh parsley, chopped
1 egg beaten
1 cup cornmeal
2 tsp baking powder
½ cup grated cheddar cheese
⅓ cup black olives, sliced

(Many small children do not care for onions, garlic, and chili powder. You may, therefore, delete these from this recipe if you think it best.)

Saute onions and garlic in a big black skillet. Mix all the remaining ingredients (except the cheese and olives, which are reserved for the topping). Add this mixture to the skillet. Stir well. Sprinkle olives and cheese on top. Bake at 350° F. for 20 minutes.

Crunchy Soybeans

(You may want to prepare this snack during the evening to prevent the oven from heating up the school on a hot summer day.)

Cover 2 cupfuls of soybeans with water. Soak them in the refrigerator for 8 hours.* Drain beans and spread them out onto two cookie sheets. Bake in a 200° F. oven for 2½ hours. Drizzle a teaspoonful of olive oil over the beans on each sheet. Stir the beans until they are all coated with oil. Return cookie sheets to the oven for ½ hour. Remove from oven and immediately sprinkle beans lightly with salt. Cool. Store in covered jar.

Serve beans, as salted nuts, with apple slices or cold juice.

BEATRIX POTTER

"Do you know the story of Peter Rabbit? Well, it was written by a woman named Beatrix Potter. She wrote it for a little friend who was sick in bed. Beatrix also wrote about Squirrel Nutkin and Mrs. Twiggywinkle and *many* other creatures. When you go to the library, ask for a few of Beatrix Potter's books—they also have good pictures that Beatrix made for us to enjoy."

---

*Have the children compare 2 soybeans, one that is dried and one that has been soaked for 8 hours.

an Afterword

Well, Sarah, we DID it! And your drawings hold it all together. I want you to know how I've appreciated your light-heartedness AND tenacity over these long months. You are a very special gift to all of us. Godspeed, S.L.

Warm thanks to my co-teachers at Little Earth School who were so generous in their emotional support while I was writing this Almanack. ¡Gracias a David Coffey, Maria da Silva, Steven Munzenrider, Ann Beneventi and Linda Hinckley! I've been so lucky to work with each of you.

Thanks to my sister, Dixie Hyde for ideas and help with the manuscript, and to Londi for reviewing it.

And now to you, dear reader, I would add that I hope you will enjoy using this Almanack for many years. Please drop me a line* I would appreciate your comments and impressions.

Warm regards,

Dana Newmann

* in care of the publisher

INDEX